P9-CCO-349

The Parent's Homework Dictionary

DA„MAND„ Promotions
Poway,   California

Dan J. McLaughlin
Creator

For the Future of the United States

Published by
DAMAND Promotions
P. O. Box 911
Poway, CA 92074

Copyright © 1997, 1998 by Dan J. McLaughlin

All rights reserved

No part of this book may be reproduced or transmitted
in any form or by any means, electronic or mechanical,
including photocopying, recording, or by any
information storage and retrieval system, without
written permission of the copyright holder.

ISBN 1 892565 10 2

Printed by Margie King

Bulk   Order   Information

Write   to:

Homework Dictionary
P. O. Box 911
Poway, CA 92074

Call:

(619) 214-4861

Fax:

(858) 513-0335

email:

danmc10@aol.com

website:

remedia.com/homework.html

Table of Contents

Language   Arts

Language Arts

Language Arts

Abbreviations

Shortened form of a word usually beginning with a capital letter and sometimes ending with a period. Some words that can be abbreviated are: titles, words used in addresses, words used in business, states, proper names, and words that have capital letters in their title.

EXAMPLES:

TV ~ Television
PO ~ Post Office
PE ~ Physical Education
CA ~ California
Amanda L. ~ Amanda Leah

Acronym

Are words that are formed from the first letter of other words as a title.

EXAMPLES:

NATO ~ **N**orth **A**tlantic **T**reaty **O**rganization

Language Arts

Adjective

A word used to describe a noun or pronoun. Adjectives tell what kind, how many, or which one.

EXAMPLES:

What Kind

The *female* tiger slept all day.

Adjective: *female*

How Many

The *two* tigers slept all day.

Adjective: *two*

Which One

The tiger on the *left* slept all day.

Adjective: *left*

Language Arts

Adjective - **demonstrative** (this, that, these, those)
A special kind of adjective used before a noun or before another adjective. It tells which one the speaker is talking about. The words **this** and **these** refer to nouns close to the speaker. The words **that** and **those** are nouns farther away.

EXAMPLES:

This (singular - just one)

This is a great hamburger!

Demonstrative Adjective: *This*

These (plural - more than one)

These hamburgers are great!

Demonstrative Adjective: *These*

That (singular - just one)

Please pass **that** large glass.

Demonstrative Adjective: *that*

Those (plural - more than one)

Please pass **those** large glasses.

Demonstrative Adjective: *those*

4

Language Arts

Adjective - **predicate**

Follows a linking verb and describes or modifies the subject.

EXAMPLE:

The story is **wonderful.**

Subject: *story*

Linking Verb: *is*

Predicate Adjective: *wonderful*

Adjective - **proper**

Formed from a proper noun and capitalized. It helps describe the noun.

EXAMPLES:

Those tigers are from India.
They are **Indian** tigers.

Proper Adjective: *Indian*

That is an **American** car.

Proper Adjective: *American*

Language Arts

Adverb

Word that describes a verb and sometimes end in *-ly*. Adverbs tell you when, how, how much, or where an action happens.

EXAMPLES:

When (later, often, next, first, etc.)

We can go to the movie **later** today.

Adverb: *later*

How (slowly, hard, fast, quietly, etc.)

The man ran **quickly** down the stairs.

Adverb: *quickly*

Where (inside, here, far, forward, etc.)

Please go **inside** and get the card game.

Adverb: *inside*

***Ending in* ly**

Leah writes **beautifully**.

Adverb: *beautifully*

Language Arts

Affix

Can be placed at the beginning or end of the base word as either a prefix or suffix.

EXAMPLE:

Prefix: un ~ happy   unhappy

Suffix: quick ~ **ly**   quickly

Alliteration

The repeating of the first sound of each word.

EXAMPLE:

<u>M</u>andy <u>m</u>ay <u>m</u>ake <u>m</u>ore <u>m</u>uffins on <u>M</u>onday.
Alliteration: *m*

Analogy

Compares different things that may or may not be directly related.

EXAMPLE:

The Dodgers and the Celtics are both very disciplined teams.

Analogy: The Dodgers are a baseball team and the Celtics are a basketball team but a comparison was made about each team being the same in the area of discipline.

Language Arts

Antonym
A word and its opposite.

EXAMPLES:

left ~ right; up ~ down; in ~ out; fast ~ slow;
right ~ wrong; good ~ bad; strong ~ weak

Appositive
A word or phrase that follows a noun and gives more information about it.   Appositives are generally set off by commas.

EXAMPLE:

Mickey Mantle, **a Yankee great**, hit 536 homeruns in his career.

Appositive: *a Yankee great*

Article (a, an, the)
A special kind of adjective used before a noun or before another adjective.

EXAMPLE:

It is time for Emilie Lynn to take **a** nap.

Article: *a*

Language Arts

Author's Purpose
When authors write a story they are trying to provide information, entertainment, or they are attempting to persuade the reader.

EXAMPLES:

1. A **newspaper** article **informs** the reader.
2. A **mystery** story **entertains** the reader.
3. An **editorial** tries to **persuade** the reader.

Autobiography
An author's story of their own life.

EXAMPLE: Underline Autobiographies

The Diary of Anne Frank

The Autobiography of Benjamin Franklin

Base Word
A word that has a prefix or suffix added to change the meaning or tense of the original word.

Remember:

Prefix is added to the **beginning** of the word.
Suffix is added to the **end** of the word.

Base Word *continued*

EXAMPLES:

happy is the base word for *unhappy*
cycle is the base word for *bicycle*
write is the base word for *rewrite*
room is the base word for *roomy*
soft is the base word for *softly*
ship is the base word for *shipment*
teach is the base word for *teacher*

Bibliography

A list of sources that credits other people for information you use in a research paper. It is important that basic data is included for each source so that the reader can trace the information back to the original material.

EXAMPLES:

Book
List in the following order: author (name: last, first), name of book, edition, city of publisher, publisher, year of publication.
See example below:

McLaughlin, D. J. <u>The Homework Encyclopedia</u>,
    2d ed. San Diego: DAMAND
    Publishing, 1997.

Language Arts

Magazine
List in the following order: name of article, magazine, date (in parentheses), and page number. *See example below:*

"Elway Finally Gets One, Denver Wins the
Superbowl," <u>Sport Illustrated</u>.
(February 6, 1998), p. 10.

Newspaper
List in the following order: author, title of article, newspaper, date (in parentheses), page and column number. *See example below:*

Davidson, Seth "USC beats Arizona State
21-14 to Win the College World Series,"
<u>Imperial Valley Press</u>. (May 13, 1998),
p. 13, col. 2

CD-ROM Database
List in the following order: name of author, publication information for the printed source (including title and date of print publication), title of the database (underlined), publication medium (CD-ROM), name of the vendor (if relevant), electronic publication date.

Scott, George C. "How to divide mixed
numbers." <u>Homework Encyclopedia</u>.
13 Jul. 1998: BL. Newsbank.
CD-ROM. Mar. 1998.

Language Arts

Internet

List in the following order: author, title of text (underlined), publication information for the printed source, publication medium (online), name of the repository of the electronic text (such as a university library, etc.), name of computer network, date of access, electronic address used to access the document preceded by the word "Available."

Fudd, Elmer. <u>That Wrascally Wabbit</u>. Ed. Fran Johnstone. Zodiac Signs. New York: Oxford, 1986. Online. U of Chapman Lib. Internet. 26 Dec. 1985. Available FTP: etext.chapman.edu.

Biography

True story of a person's life. Written by someone who knows, studied, or has interviewed the subject. Ideally, a biography includes birth and death, education, ambition, work, conflicts, relationships, and other interesting aspects of the person's life written as a unique book or paper.

Language Arts

Book - parts of

Appendix
The location where the table, charts and graphs, lists, or diagrams are listed. You can find the appendix in the back of the book.

Glossary
Contains definitions to words used in the book and arranged in alphabetical order. Glossaries are generally located at the end of the book and usually precede bibliographies.

Index
A listing of all the subjects, names, and concepts in the book arranged in alphabetical order with page numbers that correspond to the book.

Table of Contents
Usually follows the Title Page. It lists the chapter or units and gives the page numbers. Chapters are listed in the order they appear in the book.

Title Page
Usually the first printed page of the book telling the title, author, publishing company, and where the book was published.

Language Arts

Capitalization

The first word of every sentence must be capitalized. This tells the reader that a new sentence and a new thought has begun. Also required with an abbreviation and proper nouns are also capitalized.

EXAMPLES:

Also Capitalize:

The pronoun I and its contractions:

Michael Jordan and **I** went to the basketball game. **I'll** do my homework after school.

Titles or their abbreviations when used with a person's name:

Dr. **D**. **J**. **M**cLaughlin **J**r.

Proper Adjectives:

Those are **A**merican cars.

Days: **S**aturday

Months: **A**ugust

Holidays: **M**emorial **D**ay

Capitalization continued

*Names of buildings and companies:

Federal Building

Damand Promotions

*First, last, and all important words in a title:

The Monster from Myrtle Street

*All words in the greeting and first word in the closing of a letter:

Dear Dad,

Sincerely yours,

*Proper names, streets, cities, states, and countries:

Capt. Picard lives at 1701 Nomad Street.

Dallas is in the state of Texas.

Amy Frederickson was born in California.

Language Arts

Cause and Effect

Cause is why something happens and the *effect* is the result. The cause will always happen <u>first</u> and the effect will happen <u>second</u>.

EXAMPLES:

Rafael swung the bat and **hit a homerun**.

Cause: *swung the bat*
Effect: *hit a homerun*

John Elway threw a pass and it was caught for a **touchdown**.

Cause: *threw a pass*
Effect: *touchdown*

Everyone in our class received a 100% on the spelling test so we had a **pizza party**.

Cause: *100% on our spelling test*
Effect: *pizza party*

Characterization

When the author develops the traits and qualities of characters in a story. The author may include their honesty, eye color, hobbies, etc.

Language Arts

Classifying

Grouping items by choosing the things most important to the items being classified. Items can be grouped in a variety of ways.

EXAMPLE:

Dinosaurs can be classified by what they eat. One group can be carnivorous (meat eaters) and the other herbivores (plant eaters). We can put the dinosaurs in the proper group.

Carnivorous	**Herbivores**
Tyrannosaurus	*Triceratops*
Allosaurus	*Stegosaurus*
Velociraptor	*Brachiosuarus*
Ceratosaurus	*Apatosaurus*

We can also classify dinosaurs as two-legged, four-legged, by size, or habitat.

Clipped Words

Words that have been shortened. Clipped words are **not** abbreviations.

EXAMPLES:

mathematics ~ math
telephone ~ phone
advertisement ~ ad
airplane ~ plane

Language Arts

Comma (,)

A pause that helps to make a sentence clear.

EXAMPLES:

1. After introductory words (yes, well, no, etc.).
Well, will you please clean your room?

2. In a series of three or more items.
Superman, Batman, and Spiderman are all superheroes.

3. Separating two or more adjectives.
A fresh, ripe apple was on the table.

4. Before the conjunction in a compound sentence.
Some of the kids were playing ball, but other kids were eating a snack.

5. Separate nouns in a direct address.
Mandy, please help me set the table?

6. Use between a city and state.
Poway, California

7. After a greeting in a friendly letter.
Dear Nakita,

8. After a closing in a letter.
Sincerely yours,

Language Arts

Compound Sentence

Two or more independent clauses (simple sentences) joined together by a <u>conjunction or a linking verb</u>. A comma **can** be used to separate the parts of the compound sentence.

Conjunctions: *and, or, but*
Linking Verbs: *however, therefore, because, since*

EXAMPLE: *and*

There are five hundred fish in the pond.
There are twenty goldfish in the pond.

Compound Sentence:
There are five hundred fish in the pond **and** twenty of them are goldfish.

EXAMPLE: *or*

Compound Sentence: Do you want to go to the movies **or** do you want to go shopping?

EXAMPLE: *but*

Compound Sentence:
There are five hundred fish in the pond **but** only twenty are sharks.

EXAMPLE: *however, therefore, because, since*

Mars Attacks! was a good movie, **however**, more people went to see *Godzilla*.

Language Arts

Compound Subject

When two or more simple subjects are combined using a conjunction (or/and). Combine the two simple subjects in the following sentence.

EXAMPLE:

Dan will go to school. Glenda will go to school.

Compound   Sentence:

Dan **and** Glenda will go to school.

Compound   Subjects: Dan **and** Glenda

Compound Word

Two words joined together to make one word.

Such as:

volleyball = volley **+** ball

baseball = base **+** ball

classroom = class **+** room

chalkboard = chalk **+** board

freetime = free **+** time

basketball = basket **+** ball

Language Arts

Concept Mapping

This is one way to organize ideas and information. This may include outlining, story mapping, or a story web. Once ideas are organized then it is a simple matter of composing these ideas in a creative and logical sequence. Sentences should use descriptive words and terms to give the reader a mental picture.

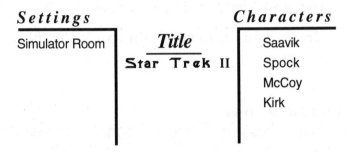

List a setting and all the characters in that setting. Describe the setting and character using colorful words (adjectives & adverbs).

Title: Star Trek II, The Wrath of Khan

Opening scene: In a simulator room depicting the bridge of the Enterprise.

Characters: Spock, McCoy, Kirk, Saavik

How many sentences can we write just with this scene alone?

Language Arts

Conflict

A problem that may pit a character against a force of nature or against another character. It may also concern a character and his or her emotions. Most movies and books have conflict.

EXAMPLE: *Conflict ~ against one another*

Batman and the Riddler were in conflict.

Conjunction

Conjunctions connect words or groups of words. Conjunctions join the parts of compound subjects, compound predicates, and compound sentences.

EXAMPLE:

Fifty students are in the class **and** twenty students are girls.

Conjunction: *and*

Common Conjunctions:

both...and; either...or; neither...nor

Language Arts

Context
It is a way you can tell the meaning of a word or term by examining the other words in the sentence. This is helpful when we don't know the meaning of the word in a sentence.

EXAMPLE:

The player used a **?** *to hit a homerun.*

By looking at the words around **?** we can tell that they are playing baseball and the baseball player hit a homerun using a **bat**.

Contraction
Two words joined together to make a shorter word using an apostrophe.

EXAMPLE:

cannot ~ can't   we are ~ we're   I am ~ I'm

Critical Thinking
To logically evaluate what is heard or read. To carefully examine the information for accuracy and recognize inconsistencies or contradictions. Test conclusions to ensure facts are backed up by evidence and eliminate faulty information.

Language Arts

Degree

Words (adjectives) that show a comparison between items. It can also make a statement about something such as a positive degree.

1. The positive degree simply describes something when there is **no comparison** being made.

EXAMPLE: August **is** a very hot month.

2. The comparative degree is used when comparing two things by adding **-er** to the adjective or using the word **more**.

EXAMPLE: August is **hotter** than May.

3. The superlative degree shows comparison of three or more things by adding **-est** to the adjective or using the word **most**.

EXAMPLE: August is the **hottest** month.

Denotation

The literal meaning of a given word.

EXAMPLE:

The denotation of the word **hurry** is to move quickly. Other words may have the same meaning. The words **rush** and **hurry** have the same meaning.

Language Arts

Dewey Decimal System

The system used by libraries to organize their books. There are 10 main categories or subject areas in the Dewey Decimal System.

000-099 **General Works** - includes reference
materials

100-199 **Philosophy** - includes psychology

200-299 **Religion**

300-399 **Social Sciences** - education, economics
law, sociology

400-499 **Language** - books, dictionaries, grammar

500-599 **Science** - astronomy, biology, chemistry,
math, physics

600-699 **Technology** - computers, medicine,
aviation, engineering

700-799 **Arts** - hobbies, music, painting, sports

800-899 **Literature** - plays, poetry, essays

900-999 **History** - biography, geography, travel

Each subject is assigned a particular area in the library within that category.

Language Arts

Dictionary

A book which gives the definition, pronunciation, origin of usage, and spelling of words. Here are the parts of the dictionary:

Definition

Gives the meaning of each word depending on the context in which it is used. Each word has at least one definition. If the word has multiple meanings then it will give each meaning and an example.

Entry Word

Entry words are shown in bold type and shows each word divided into syllables.

Guide Words

The words printed at the top of the page in a dictionary or encyclopedia. All the main entries which fall alphabetically between these two words will be on that page, guide words included.

Parts of Speech

Indicates whether the word is a noun, pronoun, adjective, verb, adverb, interjection, preposition, or a conjunction.

Pronunciation

The pronunciation of a word is given in parentheses next to the entry word. Letter symbols are used to show how a word sounds. The pronunciation key at the beginning of the dictionary gives examples of the sounds of each symbol.

Language Arts

Digraph   (sh-ch-th-wh-gh-ph)
Two letters combined to make one sound.

EXAMPLES:

Shut, **Ch**eck, **Th**e, **Wh**en, Thou**gh**, **Ph**one

Diphthong
When two different vowels are next to each other in a word and you can hear both vowels. This sound is pronounced in one syllable.

EXAMPLES:

The **-ou** sound in the word h<u>ou</u>se or the **-oi** sound in the word n<u>oi</u>se.

Encyclopedia
A set of books containing information on people, places, things, and events.

Fantasy
Something that can exist only in the imagination.

EXAMPLE:

Superman is a fantasy because a flying man doesn't exist in our world.

Language Arts

Fiction

Is something that is not true or real.

EXAMPLE:

Willie Wonka and the Chocolate Factory is fiction because it isn't true. *Independence Day* is a science fiction and *Apollo 13* is nonfiction because it really happened.

Figurative Language

Figurative language describes real items or events in an imaginative way. See similes, metaphors, personification, and idioms for specific examples.

Folk Tale

A story handed down through time from person to person. A folk tale starts out telling about real people but each time the story is told a new idea is added until it **can** become a myth. These folk tales can also be in the form of a song.

EXAMPLE:

Paul Bunyan and *The Fish Story* can be considered folk tales. The Fish Story is a good example of how the story changes over time.

Footnote

A footnote gives an explanation or the source of a quotation, fact, or idea that is used in your paper. Footnotes are indicated by a small raised number and are generally located at the bottom of the page or grouped together at the end of the chapter.

EXAMPLES:

Book (one author)

[1]D. J. McLaughlin, The Student's Homework Handbook (2d ed; Poway: DAMAND Publishing, 1997), p. 513.

Book (two or more authors)

[2]D. J. McLaughlin and C. L. Lasardi, The Parent's Homework Dictionary (2d ed; Poway: DAMAND Publishing, 1996), p. 621.

Magazine

[3]"Bugs Bunny Wins the Championship," Newsmonth (November 10, 1996), p. 10.

Newspaper Article

[4]Tomas Torres, "Yankees Win the World Series," Imperial Valley Press (December 26, 1998), p.13, col 2.

Language Arts

Foreshadowing

Hints or suggestions about what's to come in a story. We look at the setting, mood, characters actions and words, and any other information or foreshadowing from the story in order to make a predication.

Homograph

Word that is spelled the same but has a different meaning and pronunciation.

EXAMPLE:

Please **lead** the class to lunch.
The **lead** in my pencil broke during the test.

Homonym

Word that is spelled the same but has a different meaning.

EXAMPLE:

To eat a **mint** is different than the gold is kept at the **mint**.

Homophone

Words that sound alike but have different spellings and meanings.

EXAMPLES:

wear-where;   loan-lone;   hear-here

Language Arts

Idiom or Idiomatic Phrase

A phrase that has a special meaning and cannot be taken literally.

EXAMPLE:

Idiom: *It is raining cats and dogs.*

The idiom **raining cats and dogs** means it is raining very hard. Idioms cannot be understood just by the individual words and generally cannot be directly translated into another language.

Inference

When only some of the facts are given inference can find the missing information. Often times a mystery story won't give you all the information so you have to infer (guess) the missing information.

EXAMPLE:

Inference

Melissa placed the worm on the hook and then placed the hook in the water. After awhile she felt a tug on her line so she reeled it in and took a look at her hook but nothing was there.

Fishing was never mentioned in the sentences but we know that Melissa was fishing.

Language Arts

Interjection

Word or group of words that express feeling or emotion and are generally set apart from the sentence by an exclamation point (strong emotions) or a comma. An interjection usually appears at the beginning of a sentence.

Common Interjections:

Ah, Good grief, Hey, Hurrah, Oh, Oh no, Oops, Ouch, Ugh, Whew, Wow

EXAMPLE:

Wow*!* That was a great game.

Interjection: *Wow*

EXAMPLE:

Hey, look before you cross the street!

Interjection: *Hey*

Metaphor

Compares two unlike things by stating that one thing **is** another.

EXAMPLE:

Our teacher **is** a computer when she adds.

Metaphor: *teacher ~ computer*

This means that the teacher is very good at addition.

Language Arts

Modifier *(adjectives)*

A modifier describes words (nouns) in a sentence.

EXAMPLE:

The **striped** shirt was torn in the wash.

Modifier: *striped*

Myth

Are stories from ancient times that tell about the adventures and great courage of gods, goddesses, and superheroes. Hercules would be considered a myth.

Negative

A word meaning *no* or *not*. Contractions using the word **not** are also considered negatives.

EXAMPLES:

We **won't** be able to go to the zoo.

Negative: *won't*

You are **not** allowed to go to the game.

Negative: *not*

Language Arts

Nonfiction

Books containing factual information. A history book is an example of nonfiction.

Noun

Names a person, place, thing, or idea in a given sentence.

EXAMPLE:

Jennifer read a book about college.

Nouns: *Jennifer, book, college*

Noun - collective

Refers to a group of animals, people, or things in a sentence. *Group, crowd, class, family, team* are all collective nouns.

EXAMPLES:

The **family** went to the beach.

Collective Noun: *family*

Will the **team** drive with us?

Collective Noun: *team*

The **class** won a trip to Washington.

Collective Noun: *class*

Language Arts

Noun - compound

Two or more words used as a single noun. Compound nouns can be written as a single, separate, or hyphenated word.

EXAMPLES:

New York, son-in-law, baseball are all compound nouns.

Noun - plural

Names more than one person, place, thing, or idea.

EXAMPLES:

1. Nouns ending in **s, ch, x,** or **sh**... add **-es**
   (glas<u>s</u> ~ glass<u>es</u>; ben<u>ch</u> ~ bench<u>es</u>;
   a<u>x</u> ~ ax<u>es</u>; fini<u>sh</u> ~ finish<u>es</u>)

2. Nouns ending with a vowel and **y**... add **-s**
   (valley ~ valley<u>s</u>)

3. Nouns ending with a consonant and **y**...
   change the **y** to **i** and add **-es** (city~cit<u>ies</u>)

4. Nouns ending in *f* or *fe*... change the **f** to **v**
   and add **-es** to some words and just add **-s**
   to others (lea<u>f</u> ~ lea<u>ves</u>; clif<u>f</u> ~ cliff<u>s</u>)

Language Arts

Noun - plural continued

5. Nouns ending with a vowel and **o**... add **-s**
(rad**io** ~ radio**s**)

6. Nouns ending with a consonant and **o**... add
-es to some words and **-s** to others
(he**ro** ~ hero**es**; pia**no** ~ piano**s**)

7. Most singular nouns just add **-s** except for
special words such as *foot ~ feet* and
woman ~ women

Noun - plural possessive
A plural noun showing ownership. When the
plural noun ends in **-s** add an apostrophe to the
end of the word (s').

EXAMPLE:

*The cars that belong to the players are parked in
the parking lot.*

Change to:
The **players'** cars are parked in the parking lot.

Plural Possessive Noun: *players'*

For plural nouns that **do not** end in **-s** add an
apostrophe **s** ('s) to make it a possessive noun
(mice ~ mice's).

Language Arts

Noun - proper
Names an *individual* (particular) noun like the name of a river.

EXAMPLE:

The word **river** would be a common noun while the ***Colorado River*** would be a proper noun.

Noun - singular possessive
Shows ownership by adding an *apostrophe* and **-s** ('s) to the end of the word.

EXAMPLE:

The tiger has big teeth.

Change to: The **tiger's** teeth are big.

Singular Possessive Noun: *tiger's*

Objects - direct
Follows the action verb in a sentence. The direct object is a noun or pronoun in the predicate that receives the action of the verb.

EXAMPLE:

The boy steers the red **bike**.

Verb: *steers*

Direct Object: *bike*

Language Arts

Object - indirect

The direct object receives the action while the indirect object tells who or what was affected by the action.

EXAMPLE:

The pitcher threw the ball to the **catcher**.

Action Verb: *threw*

Direct Object: *ball*

Indirect Object: *catcher*

Onomatopoeia

The use of words that imitate or copy sounds.

EXAMPLE:

To say **rrrrrrrace** car would sound like the revving of a race car engine.

To say that an engine **purrrrrrrred** would mean that the engine was running in a smooth and quiet manner.

Language Arts

Outlining

There are several outline patterns, however, the example given below is the most common outline used in our school system.

1. Begin your outline with a title for the subject.

2. Arrange your main topics in a logical order.

3. Use Roman numerals in front of the main topics: I-II-III-IV-V-VI and so on.

4. Use capital letters for each subtopic.

5. Use Arabic numbers for each detail.

<u>Rules</u>

If you have a **I** then you have to have a **II**, if you have an **A** there has to be a **B**, etc. Capitalize the first word in each main topic, subtopic, and detail.

Writing using the outline

It is easier to get your learner to write an outline then it is to write a paper. However, once they organize their thoughts it is very easy to write a paper. Look at the sample outline on the next page of Michael Jordan (detail). Once they write several details about a subtopic the rest is easy!

Sample Sentences:

Michael Jordan is one of the greatest basketball players ever! He has helped the Bulls win five championships in the last six years. He has also been an all-star 10 times and he has won the scoring title seven times.

Three sentences just from one detail!

Language Arts

Outlining sample

Sports Greatest Teams
(Title of Subject)

Main Topic **I. Basketball**
    Subtopic   **A.** *Chicago Bulls*

        Detail   **1. Michael Jordan**
        Detail   **2. Bob Love**

    Subtopic   **B.** *Boston Celtics*

        Detail   **1. Larry Bird**
        Detail   **2. Bill Russell**

Main Topic **II. Baseball**
    Subtopic   **A.** *Los Angeles Dodgers*

        Detail   **1. Steve Garvey**
        Detail   **2. Sandy Koufax**

    Subtopic   **B.** *New York Yankees*

        Detail   **1. Mickey Mantle**
        Detail   **2. Lou Gehrig**

Main Topic **III. Football**
    Subtopic   **A.** *Oakland Raiders*

        Detail   **1. Kenny Stabler**
        Detail   **2. Marcus Allen**

    Subtopic   **B.** *Miami Dolphins*

        Detail   **1. Dan Marino**
        Detail   **2. Bob Grease**

Just continue to follow the format!

Language Arts

Overgeneralization

A very broad statement that does not follow the facts.

EXAMPLE:

Our teacher said that she liked basketball. A good example of overgeneralization would be to say that **all teachers like basketball**. This cannot be determined from the information on just one teacher!

Paragraph & Supporting Details

A group of sentences telling about the same idea. Each paragraph should have a topic sentence and supporting details. The main idea should be supported by the sentences in the paragraph.

EXAMPLE:

The aircraft carrier Enterprise is one of the largest ships in our navy. It can carry as many as 100 aircraft and over 5,000 men. The top speed of this massive ship is over 30 miles per hour. It generates enough electricity to light a city. On any given day more than 3,000 hamburgers, 2,000 eggs, and 1,000 hotdogs are eaten on board ship.

Main Idea: *The Enterprise*

Paragraph & Supporting Details   continued

Supporting Details:

*large ship

*carry as many as **100** aircraft and over **5,000** men

*top speed over **30** miles per hour

*generates enough electricity to light a city

***3,000** hamburgers, **2,000** eggs, and **1,000** hotdogs are eaten

When writing a paragraph on any subject all you need to do is organize your main ideas and supporting details.   Once you organize your ideas use descriptive words to describe the details. For example, instead of saying: *"This ship goes fast"*

we said

"The top speed of this massive ship is over 30 miles per hour."

Which sentence do you prefer?

Language Arts

Participle

Verb form that can function as either a verb or adjective.

EXAMPLES:

<u>Verb</u>	<u>Present Participle</u>	<u>Past</u>	<u>Past Participle</u>
paint	is painting	painted	has painted
plan	is planning	planned	has planned
play	is playing	played	has played

Parts of Speech (see individual words for examples)

Adjective
A word that tells what kind, how many, or which one.

Adverb
A word that tells where, when, how, or how much.

Conjunction
A word that connects words or a group of words.

Interjection
A word that expresses a strong feeling and is set apart from the sentence by a comma or exclamation point.

Language Arts

Parts of Speech continued

Noun
A word that names a person, place, idea, or thing.

Preposition
A word that shows a relationship between a noun and another word in the sentence.

Pronoun
A word that takes the place of a noun or nouns.

Verb
A word that shows action or links the subject to a word or phrase that tells about the subject.

Personification
Gives objects human qualities.

EXAMPLES:

The computer has a mind of its own.

The car is being stubborn!

The computer really doesn't have a mind and a car can't be stubborn.

Language Arts

Poetry

Haiku is a short Japanese poem. Haiku usually follows a pattern of three lines with seventeen syllables. The first line has five syllables, the second line has seven, and the third line has five.

Limerick is a nonsense poem that has five lines of special rhymes or rhythm schemes.

Sonnet is a fourteen line poem of a set rhyme scheme and movement.

Repetition is simply repeating words or phrases over and over again. This type of poem is designed to emphasize the main idea and assist the reader in remembering that idea.

Predicate

Tells what the subject is or what it does (the verb).

EXAMPLE:

The driver **steers** the big bus.

Subject: *driver*

Predicate: *steers*

Language Arts

Predicate - **complete**

All the words that make up the predicate.

EXAMPLE:

The capital of Utah is Salt Lake City.

Complete Predicate: *is Salt Lake City*

Predicate - **compound**

When two or more simple predicates are combined in a sentence using a conjunction (and/or). Combine the two simple predicates in the following sentences:

EXAMPLE:

The girls stood at the game.
The girls watched the game.
The girls **stood and watched** the game.

Compound Predicate: *stood and watched*

Prefix

Letters added to the beginning of words to change the meaning or tense.

EXAMPLES:

re ~ make   **re**make
un ~ known   **un**known

Language Arts

Preposition

Word that shows the relationship (where something is at) between a noun or pronoun and other words in the sentence.

EXAMPLE:

Lisa found the book **under** the chair.

Preposition: *under*

Preposition - *object of the*

Noun or pronoun that follows the preposition.

EXAMPLE:

Billy found the book under the **chair**.

Object of the Preposition: *chair*

Under is the preposition because it shows a relationship between Billy and the chair. So, *chair* must be the object of the preposition.

Prepositional Phrase

Is made up of the preposition, the object of the preposition, and all the words in between.

EXAMPLE:

Billy found the book **under the chair**.

Preposition: *under*
Object of the Preposition: *chair*
Prepositional Phrase: *under the chair*

Language Arts

Pronoun

A word that takes the place of a noun or nouns. Pronouns include *I, we, they, she, he, you, me, it, us, them, him,* and *her.*

EXAMPLES:

Ms. McMahan went to the restaurant yesterday.
She went to the restaurant yesterday.

Pronoun: *She*
She replaces the name *Ms. McMahan.*

Al and *Peggy* went to the beach yesterday.
They went to the beach yesterday.

Pronoun: *They*
They replaces the names *Al* and *Peggy.*

Pronoun - object

Can replace nouns used **after** verbs or **after** words such as: *to, for, with, in, at.*

Object Pronouns: *me, you, he, her, it, us, them*

EXAMPLE:

Lisa waved *to* the *crowd.*
Lisa waved *to* **them**.

Verb: *waved*

Object Pronoun: *them*

Language Arts

*Pronoun - **possessive***

A possessive pronoun can replace a possessive noun. Some possessive pronouns appear before a noun. Use *my, your, his, her, its, our,* and *their* before nouns in a sentence.

EXAMPLES:

His story will be printed in the newspaper.
Possessive   Pronoun: *His*

Please give back **my** baseball.
Possessive   Pronoun: *my*

That ball is **mine**!
Possessive   Pronoun: *mine*

Our car has a dent in the fender.
Possessive   Pronoun: *Our*

Punctuation

Apostrophes (') - Are used to form possessive singular nouns (teacher's), plural nouns that end in -*s* (Torres'), plural nouns that don't end in -*s* (women's), and in contractions to replace dropped letters (they will ~ they'll).

End Marks - At the end of a sentence. A period (.) ends a declarative or imperative sentence, a question mark (?) ends a question, and an exclamation point (!) ends an exclamation.

Language Arts

Punctuation continued

Colon (:) - Can be used after a greeting in a business letter, before a list, or to join two complete sentences.

Comma (,) - see Comma

Quotation Marks (" ") - Used to show a person's exact words.

Semicolon (;) - A strong comma to separate phrases, titles, or names with addresses.

Quotation

Direct - Gives a speakers exact words. Exact quotes are capitalized and have quotation marks at the beginning and end of the quote.

EXAMPLE:

"Always do your best," said the teacher.

Indirect - States what a person said without using their exact words.

EXAMPLE:

The teacher said to do our best.

Language Arts

Sentence

A group of words that express a complete thought. The sentence must contain a subject and a predicate.

EXAMPLE:

_{subject}   _{predicate}
Elmo likes to be tickled on the tummy.

Sentence - *declarative*

Makes a statement and ends with a period.

EXAMPLE:

The first day of practice is always the hardest.

Sentence - *exclamatory*

Expresses strong feelings and ends with an exclamation point.

EXAMPLE:

She is a great mom!

Sentence - *imperative*

Gives a command or makes a request and ends with a period.

EXAMPLE:

Don't run on the bus. Please check your binder.

Language Arts

Sentence - *fragment*

A group of words that do not express a complete thought or does not have a subject and/or a predicate.

EXAMPLE:

Complete Sentence:
Kermit and Miss Piggy went to the beach.

Sentence Fragment: *went to the beach*

The words do not make a complete sentence because the subject (who or what) is missing.

Sentence - *interrogative*

Asks a question and ends with a question mark.

EXAMPLE:

When will Mandy arrive at college?

Simile

Compares two things by stating that one item *is like* another.

EXAMPLE:

The **runner** runs **like** the **wind**.

Simile: runner ~ wind

This just means that the runner is fast.

Language Arts

Subject

Tells whom or what the sentence is about.

EXAMPLE: Hint - Look for the noun!

The **tiger** slept all day.

Subject: *tiger*

Subject - *complete*

All the words (modifiers) that make up the subject.

EXAMPLE:

The coach and the quarterback waved to the crowd.

Complete Subject:
The coach and the quarterback

Subject - *simple*

The most important word or words in the complete subject.

EXAMPLE:

The **girls** at the school play softball.

Complete Subject: *The girls at the school*
Simple Subject: *girls*

Language Arts

Subject ~ Verb Agreement
When there is a *singular* subject there must be a *singular* verb. When there is a *plural* subject there must be a *plural* verb. This means the subject and verb agree in number.

EXAMPLES:

The <u>student</u> <u>is</u> a fast runner.
The <u>students</u> <u>are</u> fast runner<u>s</u>.

<u>He</u> <u>is</u> a fast runner.
<u>They</u> <u>are</u> fast runner<u>s</u>.

<u>Ms. Przytula</u> <u>is</u> a good teacher.
<u>Mr. Mac</u> and <u>Ms. Przytula</u> <u>are</u> good teacher<u>s</u>.

<u>Uncle Woodrow</u> <u>was</u> a WWII hero.
<u>Uncle Woodrow</u> and <u>Dr. Gaynor</u> <u>were</u> WWII hero<u>es</u>.

Subordinate Clause
A group of words that contain both a subject and a predicate. A clause can be part of a sentence. Every sentence contains at least one clause.

EXAMPLE:

<u>The balloon floated</u> into the air.

Subject: *balloon*
Predicate: *floated*
Clause: *The balloon floated*

54

Language Arts

Suffix

A suffix is added to the end of a base word.

EXAMPLE:

		base word	suffix
wearable	=	wear	~ *able*
basement	=	base	~ *ment*
played	=	play	~ *ed*

Summarizing

A way of condensing information using only the key points. The opening sentence should give a clear description of the main idea. The rest of the summary should support the main idea in as few words as possible without changing the meaning. The summary must be in sequence with the story.

1. Tell about the main setting, characters, and the plot.

2. State any major conflicts and how that conflict came into being a conflict.

3. Finish with how the story or movie ended and how the conflict was solved.

Language Arts

Syllabication

A way of dividing words into syllables usually seen in dictionaries.

EXAMPLE: syl-la-bi-ca-tion

Rules: *For dividing words into syllables.*

1. Affixes

When a word has an affix (prefix or suffix) divide between the root word and affix:
Prefix: **re ~ write**   *Suffix:* **help ~ ful**

2. Compound   Words

Divide between the two words: **foot ~ ball**

3. Double   Consonants

When a word has double consonants divide between the double consonants: **bub ~ ble**

4. Two   Consonants

When two consonants are between two vowels divide between the consonants:
sis ~ ter

5. One   Consonant

When one consonant is between two vowels divide the word between the first vowel and the consonant: **spo ~ ken**

Language Arts

Syllabication continued

6. Ending in LE
When a consonant is followed by -LE divide the word before the consonant: **ta ~ ble**

7. X
When the letter x is between two vowels divide the word after the x: **ox ~ en**

Synonym
Words that have similar meaning.

EXAMPLE:

The word <u>talk</u> has the following synonyms:

Please **speak** to the teacher.
Please **yell** to the teacher.
Please **relate** to the teacher.
Please **explain** to the teacher.
Please **convey** to the teacher.

Tense - future
A verb that tells what will happen in the future by using the helping verbs *will* or *shall*.

EXAMPLES:

Elaine **will** bring her new car to the parade.

Future Tense: *will*

Language Arts

Tense - *past*

A verb that shows what has already happened.

EXAMPLE:

Stephanie **liked** her grandmother's pie.

Past Tense: *liked*

Rules: (For forming past tense)

1. Most verbs add **-ed** (play-played)

2. Verbs ending with *e*...add **-d** (hope-hoped)

3. Verbs ending with a consonant and *y* change the *y* to *i* and add **-ed** (study-studied)

4. Verbs ending with a single vowel and a consonant just double the final consonant and add **-ed** (stop-stopped)

Tense - *present*

A verb that shows action as it is happening.

EXAMPLE: The teacher **sees** the students.

Present Tense: *sees*

Rules: (For forming present tense)

Add *-s* when the verb is singular and do not change the verb with plural subject or with the pronouns *I* and *you*.

Language Arts

Titles

The first, last, and all the important words capitalized in the title. Printed titles of books, magazines, newspapers, and movies should appear in italics or underlined. Quotation marks should be used for songs, articles, book chapters, poems, and titles of short stories. Do not capitalize words such as: *the, a, in, and, or of,* unless they begin or end the title.

EXAMPLE: Movie Title

R eturn of the J edi

Topic

The subject of each sentence, paragraph, or story. Each sentence will have a topic (subject).

EXAMPLE:

The **tiger** is a large and beautiful animal. However, you would not want **one** as a house cat. **It** can weigh several hundred pounds and can eat $40 of meat each day.

Topic: *Tiger*

Because each sentence tells something about a tiger.

Language Arts

Topic Sentence and Main Idea
The first sentence that best describes the main idea of a paragraph. The topic sentence is then supported by details.

EXAMPLE: *Read the following paragraph*

The aircraft carrier Constellation is one of the largest ships in our navy. It can carry up to 100 aircraft and over 5,000 men. The top speed of this massive ship is over 30 miles per hour. It can also generate enough electricity to light a city.

Main Idea: Constellation

Topic Sentence:
The aircraft carrier Constellation is one of the largest ships in our navy.

The rest of the supporting sentences tell something about the Constellation!

Verb
Action word that tells what the subject does or did.

EXAMPLE:

The ball **flew** over the fence.

Subject: *ball*
Verb: *flew*

Language Arts

Verb - *helping or auxiliary*

Works with the main verb to form a verb phrase. Helping verbs do not show action.

EXAMPLE:

Mandy **is** winning the race.

Helping Verb: *is*

Common Helping Verbs:
has-have; is-are; will-shall; must-ought; can-could; should-would; do-did

Verb - *irregular*

Verbs that *do not* need *-d* or *-ed* to show that something has already happened.

EXAMPLES:

Verb ~ *Irregular Verb*

bring ~ *brought*	come ~ *came*
go ~ *went*	make ~ *made*
run ~ *ran*	say ~ *said*
take ~ *took*	think ~ *thought*
write ~ *wrote*	ring ~ *rang*
sing ~ *sang*	swim ~ *swam*
begin ~ *began*	tear ~ *tore*
wear ~ *wore*	break ~ *broke*
speak ~ *spoke*	steal ~ *stole*
choose ~ *chose*	freeze ~ *froze*
blow ~ *blew*	grow ~ *grew*
know ~ *knew*	fly ~ *flew*

Verb - linking

Links the subject of the sentence with a word or words in the predicate. A linking verb does not show action and is not a helping verb. It is also followed by a word in the predicate that names or describes the subject.

EXAMPLE:

Jenny **was** a <u>teacher</u>.

Linking Verb: *was*

Common Linking Verbs: am, was, are, is, were, be, look, feel, taste, smell, seem, appear

Verb Phrases

Made up of a main verb and a helping verb.

EXAMPLE:

Mandy **is winning** the race.

Verb Phrase: *is winning*

Verb - regular

Shows past tense by adding **-d** or **-ed** to the end of the word.

EXAMPLES:

jump ~ jumped   leap ~ leaped   type ~ typed

Language Arts

*Verb - **transitive***

When <u>someone</u> or <u>something</u> in the predicate receives that action.

EXAMPLE:

The students **cheered** the *principal*.

Transitive Verb: *cheered*

Direct Object: *principal*
(the principal received the action)

Vowel Rules

Most words in the English language follow rules just like students follow rules in their classroom. Vowels and consonants are put together to make words. The words are sounded out by where each vowel and consonant is placed in that word. If you follow the rules below it will help you sound out most words in our language.

C stands for consonant
V stands for vowel

1. CVVC

When two vowels are together you hear only the first long vowel sound.

Example: **meat**

Vowel Rules continued

2. **VCV**

When a consonant is between two vowels and the last vowel is an -e the first vowel has a long vowel sound.

Example: **ate**

3. **VCCCV**

When two or more consonants are between two vowels the first vowel has a short vowel sound.

Example: **apple**

4. **CVC**

When a vowel is between two consonants the vowel sound is short.

Example: **cup**

5. **CV**

When a vowel follows a consonant in a two letter word the vowel is long.

Example: **so**

Language Arts

Word Connotations

A word that suggests meaning in addition to its definition. Connotations can be positive, negative, or neutral.

EXAMPLE:

Kenny Stabler threw a long pass that was dropped in the end zone and we just sat there, *marveling*.

The word *marveling* could mean:

1. Marveling can have a *positive* meaning in that we were delighted at the dropped pass.

2. It can have a *negative* meaning in that we were staring in displeasure at the dropped pass.

3. It can also have a *neutral* meaning in that we just watched the event.

Writing Process

Prewriting

Done before any writing takes place. Brainstorm a list of ideas about the topic. Use this list to discuss ideas with fellow classmates. Once a list has been decided upon gather information on the items/subject. Consider the audience that will read or hear your words. This will assist you in using the correct vocabulary for the audience.

Language Arts

Writing Process continued

Drafting
Organize your thoughts on paper. Place the ideas in a logical sequence and develop each one to write a first draft. Have others read your paper and offer suggestions.

Revising
This is the time to improve on original ideas. Rearrange your ideas and words to fit the writing and take out or add parts that will help make it a better paper. Complete any unfinished ideas and replace overused or unclear words.

Proofreading
Examine the paper for grammar and punctuation. Look for words that are used out of context or incorrectly. After these corrections are made have someone read it again. Copy it again, making all the corrections. Make sure it is a neat paper!

Publishing
Now you can share your final paper. Remember, neatness counts! Bind your work so that it is appealing. Illustrate the cover or different parts so that the reader can better understand the story. Always remember that mental image you want your readers to have of your writing.

Language Arts

Writing (parts of a story)

Plot
Beginning - State the opening problem
Middle - State the consequences of the problem
End - State how the problem was solved

Setting
The time and the place of the story. Provide clues for the reader to make conclusions or be descriptive. Give a mood of the characters or their surroundings.

Characters
Can be animals, people, or imaginary beings.

Writing Made Easy
Believe it or not, writing can be easy if we follow two simple rules.

1. Make the sentences interesting, relevant, and in sequence.

2. Organize your thoughts in sequence and in the given format (summary, biography, story, etc.).

Here is the assignment: Have your child write a paragraph about what they did this weekend. How much will they write?????

Language Arts

EXAMPLE:

I went to the movies with my friend. My family went out to dinner Saturday night. I played a game with my brother. We went to grandma's house Sunday morning.

Have you seen this style of writing before? Some students may have difficulty expressing themselves in writing. Writing is hard work to them but maybe we can do something to give the paper feeling and make it easier. Now let's take a look at this paragraph one sentence at a time. We will add some colorful words (adjectives and adverbs) to make each sentence more interesting so that the reader will have a mental image of the writing.

Sentence One:

I went to the movies with my friend.

How about this instead:

Bobby and *I* went to see a *fantastic* movie Friday night. The movie was about *aliens* from another planet *trying to take over the world* and it was called *Independence Day.*

Difference:

We now have two sentences telling the reader who went to the movie, what they saw, the plot, and how they felt about the movie (fantastic).

Language Arts

Sentence Two:

My family went out to dinner Saturday night.

How about this instead:

After a *long day of shopping* on Saturday my family went to eat *hamburgers* at *Crustiburgers*. The *hamburgers* were *good* but the *fries* were *cold!*

Difference:
Now we know that the writer didn't like his/her day of shopping (long day), what and where they ate, and a description of the food.

Sentence Three:

I played a video game with my brother.

How about this instead:

After we got home my brother wanted to play a video game. He *bothered me for 30 minutes* until I finally said okay. We played a quick game of football and *I beat him 13-10*.

Difference:
The writer really didn't want to play a game. However, he/she did play football and won.

Language Arts

Sentence Four:

We went to grandma's house Sunday morning.

How about this instead:

We got up *early* Sunday morning and went to grandma's house.

Difference:

This new sentence tells the reader the time of day (early).

New Paragraph:

Bobby and I went to see a fantastic movie Friday night. The movie was about aliens from another planet trying to take over the world and it was called *Independence Day*. After a long day of shopping on Saturday my family went to eat hamburgers at Crustiburgers. The hamburgers were good but the fries were cold! After we got home my brother wanted to play a video game. He bothered me for 30 minutes until I finally said okay. We played a quick game of football and I beat him 13-10. We got up early Sunday morning and went to grandma's house.

This is **not** a perfect paragraph but notice how much more we have in the way of length and description!

Math

Addition

There are many ways to introduce the concept of addition. Here are a few ways to help your learner understand the process.

Introduction: Let's use baseballs to introduce the concept of addition. Once the child understands this concept we can match this to a mathematical expression (sentence).

EXAMPLE:

$$1 \ + \ 2 \ = \ 3$$

Note: Kids like to use their fingers in the beginning stages of learning addition and subtraction. Use whatever works to get the point across.

Hint: Once your child understands addition, use different items such as marbles, pennies, different colored items, or boys and girls to reinforce their new knowledge. If you allow gum or candy in your home this is always an effective way to get their attention!

For Advanced Learners

Another way to get the point across is to divide a group of items in half and make an addition problem.

3 + 3 = 6

This is a great way to introduce the concept of division and multiplication. $3 \times 2 = 6$ $6 \div 2 = 3$ etc.

Another Hint: This is a good time to use pennies because this would introduce the value of money and at the same time create interest in this concept (addition). We can also add two weeks together 7 + 7. This will reinforce the number of days in a week.

Adding Multiple Digit Numbers

When adding multiple digit numbers write the math problem in columns. Since we are introducing this concept it would be a good idea to label each place value.

It is easier for students to add when the numbers are stacked in columns (vertical format). Just remember to add two digits (one column) at a time starting with the column at the right (ones)!

EXAMPLE:

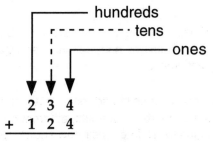

Add the ones, then the tens, then the hundreds column, etc.

```
    2 3 4
+   1 2 4
    3 5 8
```

Problem Area

It helps some learners to cover up the digits except for the ones being added together. Here is how our addition problem looks if we cover the numbers not being added.

Addition problem

```
    2  3  4
  + 1  2  4
```

Step One

```
              4    first, add the ones column
  +           4
              8
```

Step Two

```
           3  4    second, add the tens column
  +        2  4
           5  8
```

Step Three

```
        2  3  4    now, the hundreds column
  +     1  2  4
        3  5  8
```

This will help our learners breakdown a large scary problem into smaller, more manageable parts. Seeing large numbers for the first time can be intimidating!

Hint: By only adding (and seeing) two digits at a time our learners can grasp this concept more easily. If we use this same process for subtraction, multiplication, or division our learners will feel more comfortable and confident through the entire problem.

Adding (regrouping)

When adding two or more digits and the total is more than nine we need to regroup. We take the tens digit and add it to the next column.

Rules: Just follow these steps when explaining the process. It is important to follow the correct order at all times!

Step One: Add the ones together

Step Two: Regroup if necessary by carrying over the 10's digit to the next column

Step Three: Add the entire tens column

Step Four: Regroup if necessary by carrying over the digit to the hundreds column (for larger numbers)

Step Five: Add the entire hundreds column

EXAMPLE: Remember to add one column at a time starting with the ones!

```
    2  5
  + 2  7
```

Step One
```
    2  5
  + 2  7
    1  2
```
5 + 7 = 12 so we have to carry the 1 to the tens place value and regroup (add)

Step Two
```
  ►+1
    2  5
  + 2  7
  ---○2
```

Step Three
```
  +1
    2  5
  + 2  7
    5  2
```
now just add the tens column
1 + 2 + 2 = 5

75

Subtraction to check addition

Remember that subtraction is the opposite of addition and we can use subtraction to check an addition problem.

EXAMPLE:

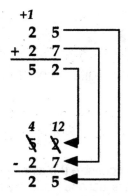

This is an excellent way for our learners to reinforce their subtraction skills at the same time prepare them for when they have to use more than one *operation* in a math problem. Meaning that there will be several functions in one equation. Such as addition, subtraction, multiplication, or division in the same equation. *See Order of Operation*

EXAMPLE:

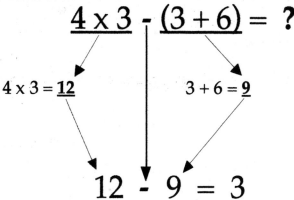

Addition Definitions

Addend

One of two or more numbers added together to find a sum.

EXAMPLE:

$$2 + 3 = 5$$

The digits 2 and 3 are addends.

Digit

Make sure to emphasize the difference between a digit and a number. A digit is just one place in a number. There are three digits in the <u>number</u> **1 7 5**.

175 = the digit **1**, the digit **7**, the digit **5**

Sum

When numbers are added together their total (answer) is called the sum.

EXAMPLE:

$$2 + 2 = 4$$

4 is the sum

Subtraction

Use any items that *grab* your learners attention. An interesting item could be dollar bills. So that is what we will use to introduce subtraction.

You start with five - $1 bills	$1 $1 $1 $1 $1
Now have your <u>learner</u> take $2	— $1 $1
This is how many you have left	$1 $1 $1

Do this several times with less than $10. Once our learner has a grasp of this concept put it in writing.

$$\$5 - \$2 = \$3$$

Hint: Just like with addition, when we introduce this concept it is important to use items (manipulatives) of interest to our learner.

Mental Math: Ask your learner how much they would have left if they started with $9 and bought a toy for $2. Kids will use a mental picture to come up with an answer.

Note: Often times subtraction is referred to as the difference between two numbers. The difference between 5 & 2 is 3. Another way to look at this problem is how far is it from 2 to 5? Counting from 2 to 5 is a total of 3 or the difference!

Subtracting multiple digit numbers (sentence form)

Use the following steps for this problem:

$$35 - 14 =$$

$$3\mathbb{5} - 1\mathbb{4} = \mathbb{1}$$ *subtract the ones first*

$$\mathbb{3}5 - \mathbb{1}4 = \mathbb{2}1$$ *now the tens*

When **no** borrowing is involved this procedure should be easy. However, this is a more difficult procedure when we borrow.

Subtracting multiple digit numbers (column form)

In column form we proceed in the same manner as addition. One column at time!

EXAMPLE: ┌─── *ones*
                        ▼

$$\begin{array}{r} 3\,\mathbb{5} \\ -\ 1\,\mathbb{4} \\ \hline \mathbb{1} \end{array}$$

                        ┌─── *now the tens*
                        ▼

$$\begin{array}{r} \mathbb{3}\,5 \\ -\ \mathbb{1}\,4 \\ \hline \mathbb{2}\,1 \end{array}$$

Subtracting (borrowing)

At times, to solve a problem, borrowing is necessary. Remember, always subtract one column at a time and start with the ones!

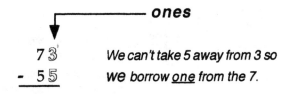

$$7\,3$$
$$-\;5\,5$$

We can't take 5 away from 3 so we borrow <u>one</u> from the 7.

Our 7 becomes 6   6 13

$$\cancel{7}\,\cancel{3}$$
$$-\;5\,5$$
$$\overline{1\,8}$$

Our 3 becomes 13, now take 5 away from 13. **Next the tens!**

Because 5 is larger than 3 we can't take 5 away from 3. The 3 has to borrow from its neighbor the 7, in the tens place value, in order to have enough. The 3 becomes 13 and the 7 becomes 6.

This is how our subtraction problem would look if it were broken down one column at a time.

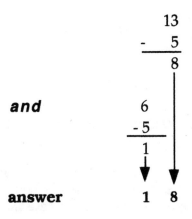

Problem Area

Subtracting with multiple zeros

This is a problem area because the usual *"borrowing from the neighbor"* rule becomes more complicated. We have to borrow from the neighbor that has money, so to speak.

EXAMPLE:

$$\begin{array}{r} 400 \\ -\ 275 \end{array}$$

We can't take 5 from 0 and when we look to the neighbor in the tens column we find another 0 so we can't borrow, <u>yet</u>. We have to move over to the hundreds column.

³ ¹⁰
$$\begin{array}{r} \cancel{4}\cancel{0}0 \\ -\ 275 \end{array}$$

The tens will first borrow from the hundreds.

⁹
³ ¹⁰ ¹⁰
$$\begin{array}{r} \cancel{4}\cancel{0}\cancel{0} \\ -\ 275 \end{array}$$

Now our ones can borrow from the tens.

⁹
³ ¹⁰ ¹⁰
$$\begin{array}{r} \cancel{4}\cancel{0}\cancel{0} \\ -\ 275 \\ \hline 5 \end{array}$$

<u>*5 subtracted from 10 = 5*</u>

⁹
³ ¹⁰ ¹⁰
$$\begin{array}{r} \cancel{4}\cancel{0}\cancel{0} \\ -\ 275 \\ \hline 2\ 5 \end{array}$$

<u>*7 subtracted from 9 = 2*</u>

⁹
³ ¹⁰ ¹⁰
$$\begin{array}{r} \cancel{4}\cancel{0}\cancel{0} \\ -\ 275 \\ \hline 1\ 2\ 5 \end{array}$$

<u>*2 subtracted from 3 = 1*</u>

answer

Note: Once we found a neighbor to borrow from remember that it will be necessary to **go back** one place value at a time.

Addition to check subtraction

Remember to use addition, the opposite of subtraction, to check the answer of a subtraction problem.

EXAMPLE:

Check

we now add 21 and 52

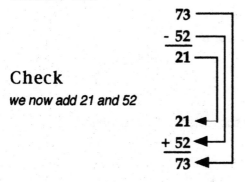

EXAMPLE:

Check

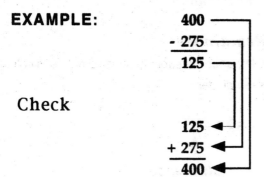

This is an excellent way to reinforce addition skills at the same time prepare students to use more than one operation in a math problem.

EXAMPLE: $4 + 2 - (3 + 1) =$ and so on....

Subtraction Definitions

Minuend

The number being subtracted <u>from</u> is the *minuend*.

$$5 - 3 = 2$$

minuend

Subtrahend

The number <u>being</u> subtracted is the *subtrahend*.

$$5 - 3 = 2$$

subtrahend

Difference or Remainder

The new number left after the subtraction is complete is called the *difference* or *remainder*.

$$5 - 3 = 2$$

difference

__Multiplication__

The opposite of division and it is also a faster way of adding.
For example, here are 4 groups with 3 in each group. Show
examples as often as possible and label whenever possible!

1   2   3   4

We can write a multiplication problem.   Four groups with
three in each group. **First**, we can write this as an addition
problem:

$$3 + 3 + 3 + 3 = 12$$

Now as multiplication problem:

$$3 \times 4 = 12 \longleftarrow \textbf{\textit{total from all groups}}$$

number in each group ⬆   ⬆ *number of groups*

Product

When numbers are multiplied together the answer is called
the product.

EXAMPLE:

$$2 \times 5 = 10$$

10 is the product of 2 x 5

Equality

As you might guess, *equality* is when items are equal in value. This can apply to money, time, weight, as well as numbers.

EXAMPLE:

$$\frac{1}{2} \ = \ \frac{2}{4} \ = \ \frac{3}{6}$$

All have the same value.

Multiples

A given set of numbers another number can go into evenly.

EXAMPLE:

Let's take the number 3, it has the following multiples:

$$3, 6, 9, 12, 15, 18, 21$$

because   **3** x 1 =   3

3 x 2 =   6

3 x 3 =   9

3 x 4 = 12

3 x 5 = 15

3 x 6 = 18

3 x 7 = 21

Factors

Are those numbers multiplied together to get an answer (product).

EXAMPLE: $2 \times 5 = 10$

The factors of **10** are 2 & 5 because 10 is the *product* of these two numbers multiplied together.

EXAMPLE: The factors of 24 are:

$$1 \times 24 = 24$$
$$2 \times 12 = 24$$
$$3 \times 8 = 24$$
$$4 \times 6 = 24$$

These are all the possible multiplication sentences that equal 24. So we can say that the numbers 1, 2, 3, 4, 6, 8, 12, and 24 are all factors of the number 24.

Prime Factorization

When we use only prime numbers to find a particular product.

EXAMPLE: The prime factorization for 24 is:

$$3 \times 2 \times 2 \times 2 = 24$$

2 and 3 are the prime factors of 24.
A factor tree can help you find prime factors!

Factor Tree

A factor tree is a way to find all the factors of a composite number. Using the number 10 (composite number) to show a factor tree, a student will be able to factor until there are only <u>prime numbers</u> left at the bottom of the tree.

EXAMPLES:

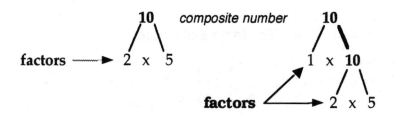

These are all the factors of 10 (1 & 10; 2 & 5)! Lets try a more complicated composite number. Notice the numbers at the bottom of the trees are prime. This will always be the case if we factor out all the numbers!

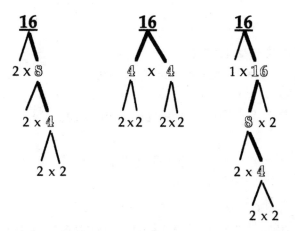

All numbers are factors of 16 (1, 2, 4, 8, 16). Again, all the bottom numbers on the factor trees are *prime numbers*!

Inequalities

When 2 numbers do not have the same value. This can be written in the following ways.

EXAMPLE:

$$3 < 4 \quad or \quad 4 > 3 \quad or \quad 4 \neq 3$$

Definition of signs: < means less than; > means greater than; ≠ means not equal to (For the purposes of this book, this just means that 4 is not the same as 3.)

Multiplying by 10, 100, 1,000

Is the same as moving the decimal point to the right or adding zeros to a given number.

EXAMPLE:

$$360 \times 1\underline{0} = 3,60\underline{0}$$

360 *becomes* 3,600

When there are no numbers to the right of the decimal point just add a zero (s) to satisfy the problem. When multiplying by 100 move the decimal point two places to the right.

$$360 \times 1\underline{00} = 36,0\underline{00}$$

Look at it this way, just add the zeros from one number to the end of the other number. Because:

$$360 \times 1 = 360 \quad and \quad 360 \times 1\underline{0} = 3,60\underline{0}$$

so

$$360 \times 1\underline{00} = 36,0\underline{00}$$

Multiplying positive and negative integers

When multiplying positive and negative integers we need to follow the chart below.

When multiplying:

A positive times a positive *the answer is*
positive

$$+4 \times +4 = +16$$

A positive times a negative *the answer is*
negative

$$+4 \times -4 = -16$$

A negative times a negative *the answer is*
positive

$$-4 \times -4 = +16$$

Just multiply as you would any other numbers and remember the rules above. *See dividing integers for more instruction.*

Division

The opposite of multiplication and a faster way to subtract. Division is when we have a large group of items that we break up into smaller equal groups. We can present this concept to our children using marbles, pennies, baseball cards, candy, etc. Have the items in one pile (group) and then do the *"one for me, one for you"* routine. This is division at its simplest form and kids can understand this concept because they have been doing it for years.

It is also important that we know a division problem when we see one.

EXAMPLE:
All the following are division problems.

$$48 \div 6 \quad \text{division}$$

$$\frac{48}{6} \quad \text{fraction}$$

$$6\overline{)48} \quad \text{division}$$

$$48{:}6 \quad \text{ratio}$$

All have an answer of 8. Even in the case of a *ratio* we must divide and in this case it would be 8:1 (8 to 1).

Because:
$$48{:}6 \ = \ \frac{48}{6} \ = \ 48 \div 6 \ = \ 6\overline{)48}$$

Division Definitions

Dividend

    Is the number that is divided by the divisor.

    360 ÷ 10 = 36.0 where 360 is the dividend.

$$10\overline{)360} \longleftarrow \textit{dividend} \longrightarrow 360 \div 10 = 36$$

Divisor

    The number that is divided into the dividend.

    360 ÷ 10 = 36.0 where 10 is the divisor.

$$\mathbf{10}\overline{)360} \qquad 360 \div \mathbf{10} = 36$$

$$\textit{divisors}$$

Quotient

When numbers are divided the answer is called the quotient.

360 ÷ 10 = 36.0 where 36.0 is the quotient.

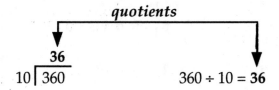

$$\textit{quotients}$$

$$10\overline{)360} \qquad\qquad 360 \div 10 = \mathbf{36}$$

How to divide

Continually follow the four step rule and you will never go wrong! Divide, multiply, subtract, and bring down.

EXAMPLE:

Divide 4 into 29

$$4\overline{)293}$$ 7

4 will not go into 2 so we move over one digit to 29 and 4 goes into 29 a total of 7 times

Multiply 7 x 4

$$4\overline{)293}$$ 7
$$-\underline{28}$$

7 x 4 = 28

Subtract 29 - 28

$$4\overline{)293}$$ 7
$$-\underline{28}$$
$$1$$

29 - 28 = 1

Bring down the 3

$$4\overline{)293}$$ 73
$$-\underline{28}$$
$$13$$
$$-\underline{12}$$

divide 4 into 13 three times

Do it all again

$$4\overline{)293}$$ 73 **r 1**
$$-\underline{28}$$
$$13$$
$$-\underline{12}$$
$$1$$

4 will not go into 1 so we have a remainder of 1

EXAMPLE: With no remainder:

$$\begin{array}{r} 6 \\ 5\overline{\smash)30} \\ -\underline{30} \\ 0 \end{array}$$

Using the same 4 step rule divide, multiply, subtract, and bring down *if necessary*.

Dividing by 10, 100, 1000

Is the same as moving the decimal point to the left.

EXAMPLE:
$$360 \div 10 = 36$$

or

$$\textit{divisor} \longrightarrow 10\overline{\smash)360} \longleftarrow \textit{dividend}$$

The decimal point is moved from 360. to 36.0 when dividing by 10. For every zero in the divisor move the decimal point one place to the left.

EXAMPLES:
$360. \div 1\underline{0}\,\underline{0}\quad = 3.60$ move decimal left **2** places
$360. \div 1,\underline{0}\,\underline{0}\,\underline{0}\quad = .360$ move decimal left **3** places
$360. \div 10,\underline{0}\,\underline{0}\,\underline{0} = .0360$ move decimal left **4** places

Hint: As the decimal point moves to the left zeros must be placed to the left of the 3 in order to make the number correct.

Multiplication to check division

Multiply the divisor by the quotient to find the dividend.

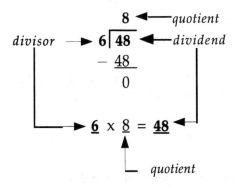

This division problem must have the correct answer because we multiplied the divisor by the quotient to find the dividend. Students often confuse the definitions for divisor, dividend, and quotient.

Dividing with different remainders

All this means is that we have some left over. We can write this as a decimal, fraction, or as a remainder. Now try $27 \div 6 =$

EXAMPLE: *Remainder as decimal number:*

```
      4.5
  6 | 27.0      Add a zero & decimal point
  − 24          to the dividend & quotient!
     3 0
  − 3 0
      0
```

EXAMPLE: *Remainder as a fraction:*

$$\begin{array}{r} 4 \quad \textbf{3/6} \ \text{(or 1/2 in lowest terms)} \\ \textit{divisor} \longrightarrow 6\overline{\smash{\big)}27} \\ -\underline{24} \\ 3 \end{array}$$

remainder $\longrightarrow$ $\dfrac{3}{6} = \dfrac{1}{2}$ *Since we can not take 6 from 3*
divisor $\longrightarrow$ *we write it as a fraction*

EXAMPLE: *Remainder as a remainder:*

$$\begin{array}{r} 4 \ \text{r}\, 3 \\ 6\overline{\smash{\big)}27} \\ -\underline{24} \\ 3 \end{array}$$

Since we cannot take 6 from 3 we say that there is 3 left over or a remainder of 3. The letter **r** stands for remainder.

95

Dividing with negative integers

At times our learners forget how to multiply, divide, add, or subtract negative integers. Remember, dividing negatives is the same as multiplying negatives for a positive or negative answer.

EXAMPLES:

Dividing *one negative* number your answer will be:

negative $^-4 \div +2 = ^-\mathbf{2}$

Dividing *two negative* numbers your answer will be:

positive $^-4 \div ^-2 = +\mathbf{2}$

Dividing with *all positive* numbers will always give you a:

positive $+4 \div +2 = +\mathbf{2}$

Dividing an *odd* number of negatives will give you a:

negative $(^-12 \div ^-6) \div (^-4 \div +2) = ^-\mathbf{1}$

Dividing an *even* number of negatives will give you a:

positive $(^-4 \div ^-2) \div (^-4 \div ^-2) = +\mathbf{1}$

Multiplying with negative numbers

Now we will check to see if multiplying the same numbers will give us a positive or negative answer. Remember, multiplying negatives is the same as dividing negatives for a positive or negative answer.

EXAMPLES:

Multiplying *one negative* number your answer will be:

negative $^-4 \times ^+2 = ^-\mathbf{8}$

Multiplying *two negative* numbers your answer will be:

positive $^-4 \times ^-2 = ^+\mathbf{8}$

Multiplying with *all positive* numbers will always give you a:

positive $^+4 \times ^+2 = ^+\mathbf{8}$

Multiplying an *odd* number of negatives will give you a:

negative $(^-12 \times ^-6) \times (^-4 \times ^+2) = ^-\mathbf{576}$

Multiplying an *even* number of negatives will give you a:

positive $(^-4 \times ^-2) \times (^-4 \times ^-2) = ^+\mathbf{64}$

Fractions

A fraction is generally know as a part of a whole such as a dime is part of a dollar or *1/10 of a dollar*. Money is a good item to use to introduce the concept of fractions. Another good way to introduce fractions is to take a piece of paper and cut it in halves or fourths. Give one piece to your child and keep the other. Explain that they have 1/2 and you have 1/2. Now write the fraction 1/2 on each piece of paper.

Whole

$$\boxed{\frac{1}{2} \mid \frac{1}{2}}$$

Denominator

The bottom number in a fraction.

EXAMPLE: In the fraction:

$$\frac{3}{4} \longleftarrow \text{\textit{denominator}}$$

The 4 is the denominator and the 3 is the numerator. This fraction means that we have 3 out of the 4 pieces left. Explain that the denominator is number of pieces we started with before any pieces were taken away.

Numerator

The top number of a fraction.

EXAMPLE: In the fraction

$$\frac{3}{4} \longleftarrow numerator$$

The 3 is the numerator and the 4 is the denominator. This means that we have 3 out of the 4 original pieces left.

Adding Fractions *(with the same denominator)*

If the denominators <u>are the same</u> simply add the numerators together. The denominator in the answer will be the same as the problem.

EXAMPLE:

$$\frac{3}{7} + \frac{2}{7} = \frac{}{7} \longleftarrow place\ first$$

Now add the numerators:

$$\frac{3}{7} + \frac{2}{7} = \frac{5}{7}$$

EXAMPLE:

$$\frac{4}{8} + \frac{3}{8} = \frac{}{8} \longleftarrow place\ first$$

Now add the numerators:

$$\frac{4}{8} + \frac{3}{8} = \frac{7}{8}$$

Adding Fractions (with different denominators)

When we add fractions with *different denominators* work to make the denominators the same. Here is what we do!

To add the fractions:

$$\frac{2}{4} + \frac{3}{8} =$$

Our first step would be to change one denominator so that it is the *same as the other*. In this problem it is easy to see that the denominator of 4 can be changed to 8 simply by multiplying by 2. What we do to the numerator we must do to the denominator!

Multiply x **2** $\dfrac{2 \times 2}{4 \times 2} = \dfrac{4}{8}$

The denominators are now the same (8) and can be added together:

now add $\dfrac{4}{8} + \dfrac{3}{8} = \dfrac{7}{8}$

Remember, once the denominators are the **same** it is just a matter of adding the numerators!!!

EXAMPLE:

$$\frac{1}{3} + \frac{3}{6} =$$

Convert 1/3 to a fraction with a denominator of 6.

$$\frac{1 \times 2}{3 \times 2} = \frac{2}{6}$$

now add $\dfrac{2}{6} + \dfrac{3}{6} = \dfrac{5}{6}$

Difficult Example: In column form

The lowest number (LCM) that 4 & 5 can go into is 20.

$$\frac{2}{5} \quad \textit{needs to be changed to} \quad \frac{2 \times 4 = 8}{5 \times 4 = 20} \longleftarrow$$

$$\text{denominators}$$
$$\textit{are the same!!}$$

$$+\frac{1}{4} \quad \textit{needs to be changed to} \quad +\frac{1 \times 5 = 5}{4 \times 5 = 20} \longleftarrow$$

$$\longrightarrow \frac{13}{20} \longleftarrow$$

Just add the numerators 8 + 5 = ⎯⎯⎯⎯⎯⎯

Complete the problem:

$$\textit{Add} \quad \frac{3}{5} \qquad \frac{3 \times ? = ?}{5 \times 7 = ?} \longleftarrow$$

$$\text{denominators}$$
$$\textit{are the same!!}$$

$$+\frac{3}{7} \qquad +\frac{3 \times ? = ?}{7 \times 5 = ?} \longleftarrow$$

$$\longrightarrow \frac{?}{?} \longleftarrow$$

Add the numerators ⎯⎯⎯⎯⎯⎯

Subtracting Fractions (with the same denominator)

Similar to adding fractions because when we have the same denominators simply subtract the numerators.

EXAMPLE:

$$\frac{4}{8} - \frac{3}{8} = \frac{1}{8}$$

101

Subtracting Fractions (with different denominators)

Remember, if the denominators are the same just add or subtract the numerator. If the denominators are different, multiply **one** denominator by a number to get the same denominator. Just like we did when we added fractions with different denominators.

Change the denominator

$$\frac{2}{4} - \frac{3}{8} =$$

$$\frac{2 \times 2}{4 \times 2} = \frac{4}{8}$$

Now we subtract $\quad \frac{4}{8} - \frac{3}{8} = \frac{1}{8}$

Now what happens if both denominators require changing? The easiest way is to multiply each fraction by the other fractions denominator.

The fraction **3/4** and **5/7** cannot be added or subtracted in their present form so here is what we do. Multiply each fraction by the others denominator. Remember, what we do to the denominator we must do to the numerator!

EXAMPLE: $\quad 3/4 - 5/7 =$

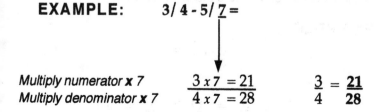

*Multiply numerator **x** 7* $\quad \dfrac{3 \times 7 = 21}{4 \times 7 = 28} \qquad \dfrac{3}{4} = \dfrac{21}{28}$
*Multiply denominator **x** 7*

Do the same to the other fraction to get the same denominator.   3/**4** - 5/7

Multiply numerator by **4** $\dfrac{5 \times 4 = 20}{7 \times 4 = 28}$ $\dfrac{5 = 20}{7 = 28}$
Multiply denominator by **4**

now add $\dfrac{21}{28} + \dfrac{20}{28} = \dfrac{41}{28} = \mathbf{1}$ 13/28

or subtract $\dfrac{21}{28} - \dfrac{20}{28} = \dfrac{1}{28}$

Complete the problem:

$$\dfrac{3}{5} \qquad \dfrac{3 \times ?}{5 \times 7} = \dfrac{?}{?}$$

same denominators

$$- \dfrac{3}{7} \qquad - \dfrac{3 \times ?}{7 \times 5} = - \dfrac{?}{?}$$

$$\dfrac{?}{?}$$

subtract numerators

Multiplying Fractions

Multiply the numerators and the denominators.

EXAMPLE:

$$\dfrac{3}{4} \times \dfrac{5}{7} =$$

$$\dfrac{3}{4} \times \dfrac{5}{7} = \dfrac{(3 \times 5)}{(4 \times 7)} = \dfrac{15}{28}$$

Multiplying mixed numbers

First eliminate the whole numbers and express as an improper fraction.

EXAMPLE: $2\,2/3 \times 1\,4/5 =$

Multiply numerators $\dfrac{8}{3} \times \dfrac{9}{5} = \dfrac{72}{15}$
Multiply denominators

Dividing Fractions

Fractions can be divided two ways, cross multiplying or inverting. Both use the same process but it is easier for kids to understand inverting (turning upside down or reversing) the second fraction.

EXAMPLE:

Using the equation:

$$\dfrac{3}{4} \div \dfrac{5}{7} =$$

We *always* invert the <u>second fraction</u> and change the ÷ sign to **X** then multiply. Look at our problem now:

$$\dfrac{3}{4} \div \dfrac{5}{7} =$$

$$\dfrac{3}{4} \times \dfrac{7}{5} = \dfrac{21}{20}$$

Cross Multiplying (follow the arrows 3/4 x 5/7 = 21/20)

$$\dfrac{3}{4} \quad \dfrac{5}{7} \quad \dfrac{21}{20}$$

104

Fractions to decimals

To find the decimal equivalent of a fraction divide the denominator into the numerator.

EXAMPLE:

$$3/4 = .75$$

Will look like this $4\overline{)3}$

Since 4 will not *go into* 3 we need to add a decimal point and zeros (as many zeros as necessary) to satisfy our division problem.

$$4\overline{)3.00}$$

First place a decimal point in the quotient (answer).

$$4\overline{)3.00}$$ *now divide*
$$\begin{array}{r} .75 \\ 4\overline{)3.00} \\ -2\,8 \\ \hline 20 \\ -20 \\ \hline 0 \end{array}$$

Divide until there is no longer a remainder (until there is zero in the answer).

Problem Area: The important thing to remember is to place the decimal point in the quotient (answer) before you start to divide. This will eliminate any problems on where to place the decimal after an answer is found.

Equivalent fractions

When 2 or more fractions are equal in value regardless of the numerator and denominator.

EXAMPLE:

$$\frac{2}{4} = \frac{3}{6} = \frac{4}{8} \quad \textit{All are half of a whole!}$$

These fractions are all equal to each other so they are all *equivalent fractions*. Each fraction just has a different number of pieces.

Improper fractions

A fraction that has a bigger (or equal) numerator than the denominator.

EXAMPLE:

$$\frac{3}{3} \quad \textit{or} \quad \frac{4}{3}$$

They are both improper fractions because they are equal or greater than one.

Note: Sometimes it is necessary to have an improper fraction, especially when we convert mixed numbers to improper fractions to multiple, add, subtract, or divide.

$$1\,{}^{1}/_{3} = {}^{4}/_{3}$$

Fractions to percent

This is the same process as converting fractions to decimals with one additional step. Divide the denominator into the numerator to find the decimal equivalent then move the decimal point two places to the right.

EXAMPLE:

$$3/4 = .75 = 75\%$$

We divide the denominator into the numerator. Since 4 will not *go into* 3 we need to add a decimal point and zeros to satisfy our division problem.

$$4\overline{)3.\underline{0\,0}}$$

First, place a decimal point in the quotient (answer) then divide.

$$
\begin{array}{r}
.75 \\
4\overline{)3.00} \\
-\underline{2\,8} \\
20 \\
-\underline{20} \\
0
\end{array}
$$

To get the percentage move the decimal point two places to the right, add a % sign and this decimal .75 becomes 75.0% (3/4 = .75 = 75.0%).

$$.75 = 75.0\,\%$$

Look at these as **equal** $\qquad 3/4 = 4\overline{)3} = .75 = 75\%$

Reducing fractions to lowest terms

Reducing a fraction means to make the existing numerator and denominator as small as possible while keeping the fraction equivalent.

Reduce to lowest terms $\frac{15}{24}$

1) Find all the factors of both numbers.

2) Find the largest common factor.

3) Divide the numerator and denominator by the largest common factor.

$$\frac{15}{24} \begin{array}{l} = 1, \mathbf{\underline{3}}, 5, 15 \\ = 1, 2, \mathbf{\underline{3}}, 4, 6, 8, 12, 24 \end{array}$$

3 is the largest or *greatest common factor* (GCF) of both the numerator and denominator.

$$\frac{15 \div \mathbf{3}}{24 \div \mathbf{3}} = \begin{array}{l} \underline{5} \\ 8 \end{array} \textit{(lowest terms)}$$

Follow these three easy step and it will always give you the lowest term of a fraction!

Lowest terms for the obvious fractions

1) First, **always** look at the numerator.

2) Will the numerator divide evenly into the denominator?

3) If it does then this is the **G**reatest **C**ommon **F**actor (GFC)!

$$\frac{3 \div 3 = \underline{1}}{9 \div 3 = 3} \qquad \frac{4 \div 4 = \underline{1}}{16 \div 4 = 4} \qquad \frac{6 \div 6 = \underline{1}}{24 \div 6 = 4}$$

Unlike fractions (also see adding & subtracting fractions)

Are fractions that do not have the same denominator.

EXAMPLE: 3/4 is *unlike* 5/7 because of the different denominators. To add or subtract these fractions we need to make the denominators the same by multiplying each fraction by the other's denominator.

$$5/7$$
$$\downarrow$$

$$\frac{3 \times 7}{4 \times 7} = \frac{21}{28}$$

$$\frac{3}{4} = \frac{21}{28}$$

Now do the same to the other fraction:

$$3/4$$
$$\downarrow$$

$$\frac{5 \times 4}{7 \times 4} = \frac{20}{28}$$

$$\frac{5}{7} = \frac{20}{28}$$

Now both fractions have the same denominator. It is now just a simple matter of adding or subtracting the numerators. Then, if necessary, we can reduce to lowest terms.

now add $\quad \frac{21}{28} + \frac{20}{28} = \frac{41}{28}$

or subtract $\quad \frac{21}{28} - \frac{20}{28} = \frac{1}{28}$

Improper fractions to mixed number

An improper fraction has a larger numerator than the denominator (4/3). A mixed number is a number with a whole and a fraction (1 1/3).

To change an improper fraction to a mixed number divide the numerator by the denominator.

EXAMPLE:

$$5/3 = ?$$

improper fraction $5/3 = 3\overline{\smash)5}$ $1\,r\,2$ $= 1\,2/3$ (mixed number)
$$\frac{-3}{2}\text{ (remainder)}$$

so $5/3 = 1\,2/3$

our denominator stays the same

remainder 2 $5/3 = 1\,2/3$

our remainder is the numerator

one whole $5/3 = 1\,2/3$

our whole number

Mixed numbers to improper fractions

The opposite process of converting an improper fraction to a mixed number.

EXAMPLE: $2\,3/4 = ?$

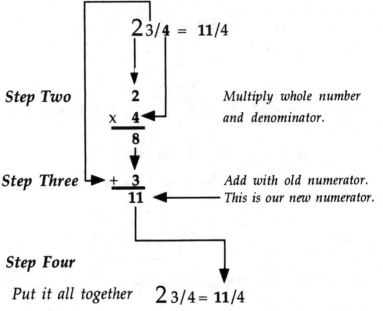

Step One $2\,3/4 = \ /4$ *Place the same denominator in our answer.*

$2\,3/4 = 11/4$

Step Two

$\begin{array}{r} 2 \\ \times\ 4 \\ \hline 8 \end{array}$

Multiply whole number and denominator.

Step Three $\begin{array}{r} +\ 3 \\ \hline 11 \end{array}$ *Add with old numerator. This is our new numerator.*

Step Four

Put it all together $2\,3/4 = 11/4$

Another Way:

Denominator **times** whole number **plus** numerator!

Follow the arrows:

$4 \times 2 + 3 = 11$

$$2\ \ 3/4 = \frac{11}{4}$$

The denominator will stay the same

Subtracting fractions and whole numbers

This can be very confusing until we convert the whole number into a common fraction. Our learner must understand that we need to have a fraction in order to subtract another fraction.

EXAMPLE:

$$1 - 3/4 = ?$$

Step One
Put in column form

$$\begin{array}{r} 1 \\ - \ \ 3/4 \\ \hline \end{array}$$

Step Two

$$\begin{array}{r} 1 \\ - \ \ 3/4 \\ \hline /4 \end{array}$$

We know our answer will have a 4 as the denominator because our problem has a 4 in the denominator.

Step Three
*Borrow from the whole number to make a fraction with the **same** denominator.*

$$\begin{array}{r} \overset{0}{1} = 4/4 \\ - \ \ 3/4 \\ \hline /4 \end{array}$$

The 1 changes to 0 and makes a fraction of 4/4.

Now just subtract numerators then whole numbers, if necessary.

$$\begin{array}{r} 4/4 \\ - \ \ 3/4 \\ \hline 1/4 \end{array}$$

112

Fraction Chart

1/2	=	.50	=	50%	=	$.50
1/3	=	.33	=	33%	=	$.33
1/4	=	.25	=	25%	=	$.25
1/5	=	.20	=	20%	=	$.20
1/6	=	.165	=	16.5%	=	$.17
1/7	=	.142	=	14%	=	$.14
1/8	=	.125	=	12.5%	=	$.13
1/9	=	.111	=	11%	=	$.11
1/10	=	.10	=	10%	=	$.10
1/11	=	.0909	=	9%	=	$.09
1/12	=	.083	=	8.3%	=	$.08
1/13	=	.076	=	7.6%	=	$.08
1/14	=	.071	=	7.1%	=	$.07
1/15	=	.066	=	6.6%	=	$.07
1/16	=	.062	=	6.2%	=	$.06
1/17	=	.058	=	5.8%	=	$.06
1/18	=	.055	=	5.5%	=	$.06
1/19	=	.052	=	5.2%	=	$.05
1/20	=	.05	=	5%	=	$.05

Decimals

Decimals are like fractions because it is a way of expressing the concept of a *part of one*. As the numbers move to the right of the decimal point the place value becomes smaller.

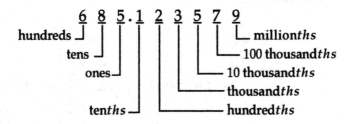

Problem Area
Our learners confuse whole number place value with decimal place value because of the similarity. Also, decimals are confusing because they start with the ten**ths** place value and not the ones place value. Teach your learner the meaning of the letters -th and that it means *part of* which also means it is on the right side of the decimal point.

Adding Decimals
Is no different then adding whole numbers. The trick is to keep each number in the proper place value (in straight columns).

EXAMPLE:

```
                                        +1  +1
        1 . 8 9                      1 . 8 9
      + 2 . 4 7                    + 2 . 4 7
         . ◄──── place first        4 . 3 6   now just add
```

Hint: Make sure the decimal points of all the numbers being added are in line (underneath) with one another. Next, place the decimal point in your answer in line with the decimal points in your problem before adding the numbers.

114

Subtracting Decimals (no borrowing)

Is the same as subtracting whole numbers. Always put the decimal point in the answer first, keep the decimal points in line, and do one column at a time.

EXAMPLE:

```
  2 . 4 7
- 1 . 3 2                2 . 4 7
   . ◄—— place first    - 1 . 3 2   now subtract
                         1 . 1 5
```

The same problem can be shown to our learners subtracting one column at a time:

from right to left

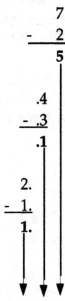

```
          7
      -   2
          5

     .4
   - .3
     .1

   2.
 - 1.
   1.
```

the answer is   **1. 1 5**

Subtracting Decimals (borrowing)

Same as borrowing when subtracting whole numbers. Place the decimal point in the answer before beginning to subtract.

EXAMPLE:

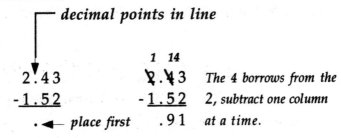

decimal points in line

$$
\begin{array}{r}
2.43 \\
-\,1.52 \\
\hline
.
\end{array}
\qquad
\begin{array}{r}
{}^{1}\;{}^{14} \\
\not{2}.\not{4}3 \\
-\,1.52 \\
\hline
.91
\end{array}
$$

place first

The 4 borrows from the 2, subtract one column at a time.

Multiplying Decimals

This can be very confusing to our learners because of the decimal placement. Just remember how many decimal places we are multiplying together. If we multiply:

$$
\begin{array}{r}
.7 \\
\times\,.4 \\
\hline
.28
\end{array}
$$

One decimal place
One decimal place
Two decimal places

We can see there is one decimal place value in each number (.<u>7</u> and .<u>4</u>) so our answer will contain two decimal places (.<u>2</u> <u>8</u>).

A common mistake:

$$
\begin{array}{r}
.7 \\
\times\,.4 \\
\hline
2.8
\end{array}
$$

One decimal place
One decimal place
Only one decimal place

There should be two!

Another common mistake:

This occurs when multiplying a whole number and a decimal number. Count the total number of decimal places in the problem and put the decimal point in the product (answer).

$$
\begin{array}{r}
7 \\
\times\ .4 \\
\hline
2.\underline{8}
\end{array}
$$

One decimal place here

Only one decimal place here

Hint: Line up the digits, not the decimal points! This is different from what we learned when adding and subtracting other numbers. Lining up digits is easier than lining up by decimals.

EXAMPLE: (difficult)

$$
\begin{array}{r}
28 \\
\times\quad .35 \\
\hline
\end{array}
$$

It's much easier this way:

$$
\begin{array}{r}
28 \\
\times\ .35 \\
\hline
\end{array}
$$

Count the number of decimal places in the problem then add a decimal point in your answer!

Dividing Decimals

The easiest way to divide two decimal numbers is to change the divisor into a whole number.

EXAMPLE: $.4\overline{)\,.52}$

Change the .4 to a 4 by moving the decimal point one place to the right. We have to do the same thing to .52. Now we have this as our division problem:

$$4\overline{)\,5.2}$$

Next put a decimal point in the quotient (answer) and then divide. Remember, always line up the decimal points!

$$
\begin{array}{r}
1.3 \\
4\overline{)5.2} \\
-\underline{4} \\
1\,2 \\
-\underline{1\,2} \\
0
\end{array}
$$

More Examples:

$$.04\overline{)\,5.23} \;=\; 4.\overline{)\,523.}$$
$$.004\overline{)\,5.230} \;=\; 4.\overline{)\,5230.}$$

Note: Multiplying the numerator and denominator by 10 is the same thing as moving the decimal over <u>one</u> place to the right. This will change .4 to 4 and .52 to 5.2. When we multiply by 10 we move the decimal place one to the right in both the divisor and dividend.

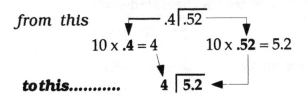

from this

$10 \times .4 = 4 \qquad 10 \times .52 = 5.2$

to this........... $\quad 4\overline{)\,5.2}$

Decimals to fractions

This depends on the value of the decimal number.

EXAMPLE:

$$.75 = \frac{75}{100}$$

First look at how many decimal places the decimal number uses. The number .<u>75</u> uses two decimal places. So this decimal can be expressed as 75 hundredths or 75/100.

We can reduce this fraction to 3/4 (lowest terms) by dividing 25 from both the numerator and denominator. The largest number we can divide from the numerator and denominator is 25. *See Reducing Fractions*

$$\frac{75 \div \mathbf{25}}{100 \div \mathbf{25}} = \frac{3}{4}$$

Notice $.\underline{2} = \frac{2}{1\underline{0}}$

$$.\underline{1}\,\underline{2} = \frac{1\,2}{1\,\underline{0}\,\underline{0}}$$

Decimals to Percent

Just move the decimal point two places to the right.

EXAMPLE: .75 = 75%

If we are converting .75 to a percentage all we need to do is move the decimal point two places to the right.

$$.75 = 75\%$$

More Examples: .751 = 75.1%

1.75 = 175%

<u>Geometry</u>

Angles

Right Angle
An angle formed at the intersection of two perpendicular lines.
A right angle measures of 90 degrees.

Acute Angle
An angle that measures from 0 degrees to less than 90 degrees.

Obtuse Angle
An angle that measures greater than 90 degrees and less than 180 degrees.

Area (see shapes)

Line
Collection of solid dots that extends forever in both directions.

Line Segment
Part of a line that has a beginning point and an end point.

<u>Line Segment</u>

end points

Lines of Symmetry
A line that divides a figure into mirror images (exactly in half).

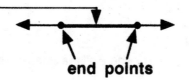

120

Perimeter

The distance around (outer area) a closed figure such as a square, rectangle, or triangle.

L = Length W = Width

$L + L + W + W$ = Perimeter

$2L + 2W$ = Perimeter

$(2 \times 8) + (2 \times 5) = 26$

Ray

Part of a line that begins at a point (called an origin) and extends forever in the opposite direction.

origin

Surface area

The amount of units necessary to cover the surface of a figure. Units can be in inches, feet, yards, etc.

Formula = $L \times W$ for a square or rectangle

L = length
W = width

area = $L \times W$

area = $5 \times 2 = 10$

Shapes

Square

A four sided shape where all the sides have equal length and four 90° angles.

area = $L \times W$

area = $4 \times 4 = 16$

Triangle

A polygon with three angles and three sides.

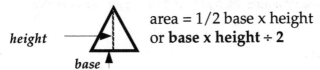

height — area = 1/2 base x height
or **base x height ÷ 2**

base

base = 4 ——— **height** = 3

$$\frac{4 \times 3}{2} = 6 \text{ (area)}$$

now divide by 2 ——►

Quadrilateral

Any four sided polygon.

Circle

A round object that has the same radius and circumference in all directions.

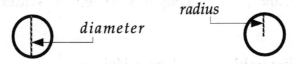

radius

diameter

circumference = $2\pi r$ or πd area = πr^2

= 3.14   **r** = radius   **d** = diameter   **c** = circumference

The **radius** of a circle is half way across the circle
from the center.

The **diameter** of a circle is the entire width of the
circle through the center.

The **circumference** is the distance around the circle.

Polygon

Any multi-sided figure that is enclosed. All squares, quadrilaterals, triangles, and hexagons are polygons.

Solids

Objects that have both length, width, and depth (3 dimensions).

Volume

The number of cubic units of a certain size that equals the space occupied by a geometric solid or *the amount of water a container will hold*. The cubic units can be any amount appropriate for measuring the volume in question. We can use gallons, wet yards, ounces, etc.

Volume Measuring

Cube Length x Height x Width *(depth)*

Pyramid $\dfrac{\text{Base x Height}}{3}$

Cylinder πr^2 x height

Cone $\dfrac{\pi r^2 \text{ x height}}{3}$

Sphere $\dfrac{4\pi r^3}{3}$

Geometry Definitions

Arc
Is the curve in any part of a circle. To find this *arc* we can use this formula:

$$(D/360) \times 2\pi r$$

If the diameter is 10 we can find the *arc*.

D = 10
π = 3.14
r = 5

$(10/360) \times 2\pi r = arc$

.0278 × 31.4 ≈ .8729

Complimentary Angle
Are two angles that when added together form a 90º angle (right angle).

angle 1 = 30°

angle 2 = 60°

so 60º + 30º = 90º

Concave
Part of a circle or shape that is curved inward.

↓*concave side*

Congruence
When two items are exactly the same size and shape. Baseballs can be considered congruent.

Convex

The part of a circle or shape that curves outward.

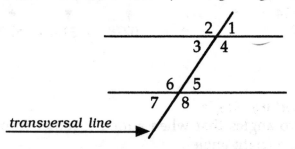

convex side

Corresponding Angles

When a transversal line intersects two parallel lines there are angles formed that are equal. These are called *Corresponding Angles.*

angle 1 = angle 3 = angle 5 = angle 7
angle 2 = angle 4 = angle 6 = angle 8

if angle 1 = 60º angles 3, 5, and 7 are also 60º
if angle 2 = 120º angles 4, 6, and 8 are also 120º

Cosine

Is the ratio of the length of the side adjacent to an acute angle of a right triangle to the length of the hypotenuse.

$$cosine \quad = \quad \frac{\text{adjacent side}}{\text{hypotenuse}}$$

Diagonals

Are lines that connect vertices (corners) of a polygon.

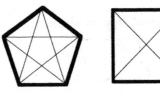

All the thin lines are diagonals!

Equilateral Triangle

Is a triangle that has three equal sides and all angles are equal to 60°.

Parallel Lines

Lines that are equal distance apart at all points along each line.

Polyhedron

A solid shape (three dimensional). Cubes, prisms, and pyramids are all examples of a polyhedron.

Reflex Angles

Are angles that measure more than 180° and less than 360°.

Rhombus
Is a quadrilateral that is slanted.

Sine
To find the sine of a right triangle we divide the length of the opposite side by the hypotenuse.

$$sine = \frac{\text{opposite}}{\text{hypotenuse}}$$

Supplementary Angle
Are two angles when added together for a 180° angle (straight line).

Tangent
The line that intersects (touchs) the circle at only one point.

Vertices
Are the corners (angles) within a polygon

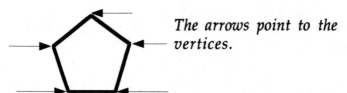

The arrows point to the vertices.

Algebra

In this section you will be able to see the basic fundamentals of the first year of algebra. Remember, this is to give the reader a basic understanding of what can be a very complex subject.

Definitions

Algebraic Expression (or just called *expression*) are those math sentences that have variables and numbers in a logical order.

Associative Property states that it doesn't matter how you add a given group of numbers they will always equal the same value.

$5 + 10 + 13 = 28;$ $(5 + 10) + 13 = 28;$ $5 + (10 + 13) = 28$

Binomials are those expressions that have ONLY two terms. $5x - 13$

Coefficient is a number that is multiplied by another number or variable. $3x$, where 3 is a coefficient of x.

Commutative Property states that no matter what order you place numbers in an addition or multiplication sentence the answer will always be the same. $2 + 3 = 5;$ $3 + 2 = 5;$ $2 * 3 = 6;$ $3 * 2 = 6$

Complex Fraction are those fractions that have another fraction as a denominator or numerator.

$$\frac{\frac{1}{2}}{\frac{3}{4}}$$

Distributive Property says that we can multiply and add terms by distributing in a given way.
$3(2 + 6)$ is the same as $(3 * 2) + (3 * 6)$ both equal 24!

Inverse Operation is a way to cancel another operation.

$$x * \tfrac{1}{3} = 9$$

To cancel out the 1/3 multiply each side by 3:

$$x * \tfrac{1}{3}(3) = 9 * 3$$
$$x = 27$$

Like Terms are those terms that have the same letters raised to the same power. $3x$ & $2x$ are like term; $3x^2$ & $5x^2$ are like terms.

Monomials are those expressions that have only one term. $3x^2$

Polynomials are those expressions that have more than one term. $x^2 + 4x + 10$

Quadratic Equation is a polynomial equation which has a squared variable. $x^2 + 8x - 12$

Rational Expression is written as a fraction.

Radicals are those that have a "root" symbol. $\sqrt{}$

Radicand is the term inside the radical sign.
$\sqrt{9x^3}$ where $9x^3$ is the radicand

Standard Form in a polynomial equation is when all terms are in descending order according to their powers and variables. $x^2 + 4x + 10$

Trinomials are those expressions that have three terms. $x^2 + 4x + 10$

Solving Linear Equations

Remember that you want to solve for the variable (unknown). First we have to isolate the variable on one side of the equal sign.

EXAMPLE:

$$3x - 10 = 26$$

Add 10 to both sides:

$$
\begin{array}{rcr}
3x - 10 &=& 26 \\
+10 & & +10 \\
\hline
\end{array}
$$

Now we have: $3x = 36$

Divide the term by 3 get have the variable (x) all by itself:

$$\frac{\cancel{3}x}{\cancel{3}} = \frac{36}{3}$$

And the answer is: $x = 12$

Another Example: Fractions

$$\frac{2}{3}x = 4$$

Get rid of the fraction multiply each side by 3:

$$\frac{3}{1} * \frac{2}{3}x = 4(3)$$

$$2x = 12$$

Divide by 2 $\dfrac{\cancel{2}x}{\cancel{2}} = \dfrac{12}{2}$

$$x = 6$$

131

Algebraic Fractions

First try to eliminate the fraction from at least one term in the equation.

EXAMPLE:

$$\frac{4x}{9} - \frac{1}{3} = \frac{x}{3}$$

Multiply each term by 9:

$$\frac{9}{1} \frac{4x}{9} - \frac{1}{3} \frac{9}{1} = \frac{x}{3} \frac{9}{1}$$

We now have: $4x - 3 = 3x$

Isolate the variable by subtracting 3 from each side:

$$4x - 3 = 3x$$
$$\underline{\quad +3 \quad\quad +3 \quad}$$

Now we have: $4x = 3x + 3$

Now subtract 3x from each side. This will isolate x on one side of the equal sign:

$$4x = 3x + 3$$
$$\underline{-3x \quad\quad -3x \quad}$$

Now we have: $x = 3$

Our answer is:

$$x = 3$$

Polynomials & Monomials (add/subtract)

Very similar to adding or subtracting regular numbers but with one difference. We need to know what we can and cannot add or subtract.

We can only add or subtract like terms. This means it must have the same variables and the same exponents!

EXAMPLE:

$$a + b - ab + 3a$$

Like Terms

We only have two "like" terms so now we have:

$$4a + b - ab$$

EXAMPLE:

$$3x^2 + 7xy - 2x^2 + 7xy$$

Now combine like terms:

$$(3x^2 - 2x^2) + (7xy + 7xy)$$

$$x^2 + 14xy$$

As you can see in this equation it is just a matter of combining like terms and adding or subtracting the numbers (coefficients). The sign (= *or* -) in front of the term will determine what to do either add or subtract!

133

Factoring GCF

Very similar to factor GCF in regular numbers. We have to find the largest number, variable, and exponent from all the terms.

EXAMPLE:
$$13a^4 + 39a^3$$

Step One: Factor the GCF from the number.
$$\mathbf{13}a^4 + \mathbf{39}a^3$$

13 is the largest factor of each number:
$$\mathbf{13}(a^4 + 3a^3)$$

Both terms have the variable "**a**" so we can factor out this variable to the smallest exponent value (a^3).

$$13(\mathbf{a}^4 + 3\mathbf{a}^3)$$

$$13a^3(a + 3)$$

Now Check:

$$13a^3 \quad * \quad a \quad = \quad 13a^4$$
$$13a^3 \quad * \quad 3 \quad = \quad 39a^3$$

$$13a^4 + 39a^3 = 13a^3(a + 3)$$

We must have it correct!

Rules to Follow

Product Rule states that when we multiply exponents together it is the same as adding them.

$a^2 * a^3 = a^{2+3}$

Quotient Rule states that when we divide exponents it is the same as subtracting them.

$\dfrac{a^3}{a^2} = a^{3-2}$

Other Rules:

$$(a^2)^3 = a^{2*3}$$

if a = 3 $\qquad (3^2)^3 = 3^6 \qquad = 729$

$$(ab)^3 = a^3 b^3$$

if a = 2 & b = 3 $\qquad (2*3)^3 = 2^3 3^3 \qquad = 216$

$$(a/b)^3 = a^3/b^3$$

if a = 2 & b = 3 $\qquad (2/3)^3 = 2^3/3^3 = 8/27$

$$a^{-3} = 1/a^3$$

if a = 2 $\qquad 2^{-3} = 1/2^3 \qquad = 1/8$

Solving Complex Fractions

Remember that a complex fraction is basically a fraction on top of another fraction. If we use the same rules for dividing regular fractions we will come up with the correct answer!

EXAMPLE:
$$\frac{\frac{1}{3}}{\frac{2}{3}} = 1/3 \div 2/3$$

We invert & multiple:

$$\frac{1}{3} \div \frac{2}{3} = \frac{1}{3} \times \frac{3}{2} = \frac{3}{6} = \frac{1}{2}$$

Follow the same rule!

$$\frac{\frac{y-3}{y}}{\frac{y-3}{2y}}$$

Remove the middle division sign as follows:

$$\frac{\frac{y-3}{y}}{\frac{y-3}{2y}} = \frac{y-3}{y} \div \frac{y-3}{2y}$$

Invert and multiple:

$$\frac{y-3}{y} \times \frac{2y}{y-3} = \frac{2y(y-3)}{y(y-3)}$$ Note the like terms! They will cancel!

Now reduce algebraically by canceling like terms:

$$\frac{2y(y-3)}{y(y-3)} = 2$$

136

Combining Like Terms

Adding all the variables (letters) that have the same power.

EXAMPLE:

In the expression

$$2x^2 + 2y^2 - x^2 + y^2$$

we combine the **x^2** and **y^2** terms

$$(2x^2 - x^2) \quad + \quad (2y^2 + y^2)$$

so now we have: $\qquad x^2 \qquad + \qquad 3y^2$

Multiplying Polynomials

The key is to multiply each term in one expression by all the terms in the other expression. Much like multiplying multi-digit numbers.

EXAMPLE: $(x + 2)(3x^2 + 2x - 5)$

Multiply the first **x** by all the other terms in the other expression: $(\mathbf{x} + 2)(3x^2 + 2x - 5)$

$$x * 3x^2 = 3x^3$$
$$x * 2x = 2x^2 \quad \longrightarrow 3x^3 + 2x^2 - 5x$$
$$x * (-5) = -5x$$

Now the **2**: $(x + \mathbf{2})(3x^2 + 2x - 5)$

$$2 * 3x^2 = 6x^2$$
$$2 * 2x = 4x \quad \longrightarrow 6x^2 + 4x - 10$$
$$2 * (-5) = -10$$

Combine like terms: $3x^3 + (6x^2 + 2x^2) + (4x - 5x) - 10$ }

Now we have: $\quad 3x^3 \quad + \quad 8x^2 \quad - \quad x \quad - 10$

Dividing Polynomials

The key is to separate each monomial.

EXAMPLE:

$$\frac{21x^2y - 12x^3y^3 - 9xy}{3xy}$$

Separate terms by monomial using the same denominator:

$$\frac{21x^2y}{3xy} - \frac{12x^3y^3}{3xy} - \frac{9xy}{3xy}$$

Now reduce to lowest terms. Keep in mind that when you divide variables it really means to subtract the exponents of each variable expression!

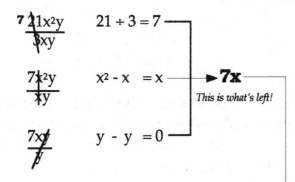

$$\frac{21x^2y}{3xy} \qquad 21 \div 3 = 7$$

$$\frac{7x^2y}{xy} \qquad x^2 - x = x \qquad \mathbf{7x}$$

This is what's left!

$$\frac{7xy}{y} \qquad y - y = 0$$

Again, do the same with the other monomials:

$$\frac{12x^3y^3}{3xy} \qquad 12 \div 3 = 4;\ x^3 - x = x^2;\ y^3 - y = y^2$$
$$\mathbf{4x^2y^2}$$

$$\frac{9xy}{3xy} \qquad 9 \div 3 = 3;\ x - x = 0;\ y - y = 0$$
$$\mathbf{3}$$

Put it all together: $\mathbf{7x - 4x^2y^2 - 3}$

138

Quadratic Equations

Solving for a variable in a polynomial equation is similar than solving for any variable. We must place all expressions to one side of the equal sign and zero on the other side of the equal sign. This is called *Standard Form*.

EXAMPLE:

$$x^2 + 2x - 15 = 0$$

Notice that all terms are in descending order (largest to smallest) according to their exponents.

$$x^2 + 2x - 15 = 0$$

Next: Factor out the variable (x) for each expression.

$$x^2 + 2x - 15 = 0$$
$$(x - \textbf{?})(x + \textbf{?}) = 0$$

Next: This is the tricky part! Finding two numbers that when multiplied together equal -15 and when added together equal +2x. The first **?** will be 3 and the second **?** will be 5.

$$x^2 + 2x - 15 = 0$$
$$(x - \textbf{3})(x + \textbf{5}) = 0$$

$$x - 3 = 0 \text{ so } x = 3$$
and $$x + 5 = 0 \text{ so } x = -5$$

solution set $x = \{3, -5\}$

Check: Now perform all the operations to check for accuracy.

$$(\mathbf{X} - 3)(\mathbf{X} + 5) = 0$$

$$x * x \quad = \mathbf{X^2}$$

Next: Multiple each *x* by the digit in the other expression.

$$(x - \mathbf{3})(\mathbf{X} + 5) = 0$$

$$x * -3 \quad = \underline{-3x}$$

Now the other *x*::

$$(\mathbf{X} - 3)(x + \mathbf{5}) = 0$$

$$x * 5 \quad = \underline{5x}$$

Now perform the operations:

$$5x$$
$$-\ \underline{3x}$$
$$\mathbf{2x}$$

Finally multiply the two digits together:

$$(x - \mathbf{3})(x + \mathbf{5}) = 0$$

$$-3 * 5 \quad = \mathbf{-15}$$

We must have factored correctly because all operations fit the equation.

$$x^2 + 2x - 15 = (x - 3)(x + 5)$$

Quadratic Equations (that do not equal zero)

Remember to write the equation in standard form (0 on one side of =) before solving for the variable.

EXAMPLE: $x^2 + 8x + 15 = 3$

subtract 3 from each side

$$x^2 + 8x + 15 = 3$$
$$\underline{\quad\quad\quad -3 \quad -3}$$

now we have standard form

$$x^2 + 8x + 12 = 0$$

Factor out the variable: $(\mathbf{x} + ?)(\mathbf{x} + ?) = 0$

Find two digits (numbers) that when multiplied together equal 12 and when added equal 8x:

How about 6 & 2: $(x + 6)(x + 2)$

Now we perform all operations to check:

$$\underline{x * x = \mathbf{x^2}}$$
$$\underline{6x + 2x = \mathbf{8x}}$$
$$\underline{6 * 2 = \mathbf{12}}$$
$$x^2 + 8x + 12 = 0$$

Sounds good to me! All are positive terms so we add all three together to check our answers. Our solution set (answer) is: $x = \{-6, -2\}$

  because $x + 6 = 0; \quad x = -6$
  $x + 2 = 0; \quad x = -2$

Solving Word Problems

The key is to give each unknown value the correct variable expression.

EXAMPLE:

If Bailey and Joseph can kick a football a combined total of 100 yards but Joseph kicks the ball 10 yards farther than Bailey. How far can each one kick the ball?

Set the variable value:

$$X = \text{Bailey's kick}$$

$$X + 10 = \text{Joseph's kick}$$

so $\quad X + (X + 10) = 100 \text{ yards}$

Now isolate the unknown value (X) on one side of the equal sign:

$$X + (X + 10) = 100$$

combine/add $\quad 2X + 10 = 100$

subtract $\qquad \underline{-10 \qquad -10}$

$$2X = 90$$

divide by 2 $\qquad \dfrac{2X}{2} = \dfrac{90}{2}$

$$X = 45 \text{ yards (Bailey)}$$

so $\qquad X + 10 = 55 \text{ yards (Joseph)}$

Rational Expressions

Add/Subtract

As with all fractions we must have the same denominator before adding or subtracting.

EXAMPLE:

$$\frac{24x}{6a} + \frac{12x}{3a} = ?$$

Multiply 3a by 2 to get 6a. Now we will have the same denominator.

$$\frac{24x}{6a} + \frac{12x * 2}{3a * 2} = ?$$

now add $\quad \dfrac{24x}{6a} + \dfrac{24x}{6a} = \dfrac{48x}{6a} = \dfrac{6(8x)}{6a} = \dfrac{8x}{a}$

EXAMPLE:

$$\frac{24x}{6} + \frac{12x}{3} = ?$$

$$\frac{24x}{6} + \frac{12x * 2}{3 * 2} = ?$$

$$\frac{24x}{6} + \frac{24x}{6} = \frac{48x}{6} = \frac{6(8x)}{6} = 8x$$

Rational Expressions
Multiply/Divide

Remember how to multiply fractions? Same thing! Multiply the numerators together and multiply the denominators. Then we take one additional step by canceling terms (reducing in effect).

$$\frac{9(x-3)^2}{7(y+8)} \quad * \quad \frac{7(y+8)}{3(x-3)}$$

Multiply numerators:

$$9(x-3)^2 * 7(y+8)$$

Multiply denominators:

$$7(y+8) * 3(x-3)$$

Put it all together:

$$\frac{9(x-3)^2 * 7(y+8)}{7(y+8) * 3(x-3)}$$

Now cancel terms: $(x-3)$ & $(y+8)$

$$\frac{9(\cancel{x-3})^2 * 7(\cancel{y+8})}{7(\cancel{y+8}) * 3(\cancel{x-3})} = \frac{9(x-3) * 7}{7 * 3}$$

Now reduce: $9 \div 3$ & $7 \div 7$

$$\frac{^3\cancel{9}(x-3) * \cancel{7}}{\cancel{7} * \cancel{3}} = 3(x-3) \text{ \emph{\textbf{is what is left}}}$$

144

Radical Expression (simplified)

We must find a way to factor out a perfect square from underneath the radical sign.

EXAMPLE:

$\sqrt{72}$ does not have a perfect square

How about: $\sqrt{36 * 2} = \sqrt{72}$

Now we can take the square root of 36 out!

$$\sqrt{72} = \sqrt{36 * 2} = \mathbf{6\sqrt{2}}$$

In the following example you take the square root of an exponents is the same dividing by 2. The key is to find a number that we can easily factor out a square root! $\sqrt{x^8} = x^4$

EXAMPLE:

$\sqrt{28x^9y^6}$ Factor the number first!

$$\sqrt{\underline{28}x^9y^6} = \sqrt{\underline{4} * \underline{7} * x^9y^6}$$

Take out the square root of 4:

$$\sqrt{\underline{4} * 7 * x^9y^6} = \underline{2}\sqrt{7 * x^9y^6}$$

Factor the variables to make it possible to take out the square root:

$$2\sqrt{7 * x^9y^6} = 2\sqrt{7 * \underline{x^8} * x * \underline{y^6}}$$

Now we have: $2\sqrt{7 * \underline{x^8} * x * \underline{y^6}} = 2x^4y^3\sqrt{7x}$

Radical Expressions (add/subtract)

You can only add/subtract radical expressions that have the same index (root) and radicand (expression under the radical sign).

EXAMPLE:

$$2\sqrt{75} - 2\sqrt{48}$$

We can simplify each expression like on the previous page.

$$2\sqrt{75} \quad - \quad 2\sqrt{48}$$

$$\downarrow \qquad \qquad \downarrow$$

$$2\sqrt{25 * 3} - 2\sqrt{16 * 3}$$

Factor out the square roots of each expression:

$$2\sqrt{\mathbf{\underline{25}} * 3} \quad - \quad 2\sqrt{\mathbf{\underline{16}} * 3}$$

$$\downarrow \qquad \qquad \downarrow$$

$$2 * \mathbf{5} * \sqrt{3} - 2 * \mathbf{4} * \sqrt{3}$$

$$10\sqrt{3} \quad - \quad 8\sqrt{3} = \mathbf{2\sqrt{3}}$$

Notice that in this example that each expression is a perfect square (25 = 5; 16 = 4) and the same radicand. Don't you wish they were all this easy!

Radical Expression (multiplying)

We must multiply coefficients and radicands separately.

EXAMPLE:

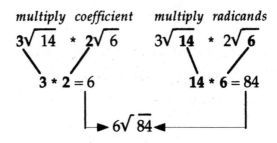

Now factor the radicand to find a perfect square:

$$6\sqrt{84} = \sqrt{4 * 21} \quad \textit{(4 is a perfect square)}$$

Take out the square of 4 (which is 2):
$$6 * 2 * \sqrt{21}$$

Multiply: 6 by 2
$$\mathbf{12}\sqrt{21}$$

This is our answer!

$$\mathbf{12}\sqrt{21}$$

Radical Expression (dividing)

Similar to other forms of division but with one extra step. We must remove the radical sign in the denominator before dividing.

EXAMPLE:

$$\frac{7}{\sqrt{5}}$$

Multiply both numerator & denominator by $\sqrt{5}$ to get rid of the radical sign.

$$\frac{7 * \sqrt{5}}{\sqrt{5} * \sqrt{5}} = \frac{7\sqrt{5}}{5}$$

Rational Exponents

Just remember the numerator of a rational exponent is the power (exponent) and the denominator is the root.

EXAMPLE:

$$81^{1/2} = \sqrt{81} = 9$$

root

$$27^{2/3} = (27^{1/3})^2 = \left[\sqrt[3]{27} \right]^2$$

exponent

Graphing

For the purposes of this book graphing is just a way of showing points (locations) much like we use longitude and latitude on a map. We use an "x" axis (up/down for east/west) and "y" axis (left/right for north/south). Our point of reference is where the two lines intersect (come together). At this intersection both axes have a value of zero.

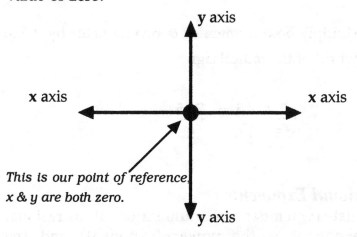

Notice the values for both x & y. The first quadrant both are positive. The second quadrant x is negative, y is positive. The third quadrant x is negative, y is negative. The fourth quadrant x is positive, y is negative.

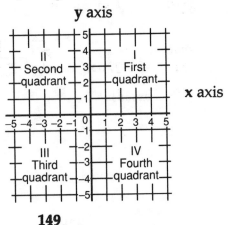

Plotting

This means to find a spot on the graph of given coordinates. Remember that the first digit of each set is found on the "x" axis (**2**, 3) and the second digit is found on the "y" axis (2, **3**).

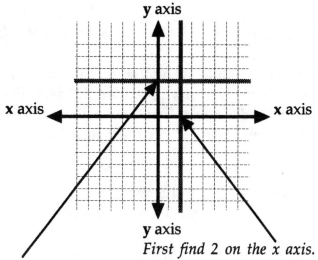

y axis

x axis   **x axis**

y axis

First find 2 on the x axis.
Now find 3 on the y axis.
Follow both lines until they intersect (meet).

Slope

Is defined as the ratio of rise (y axis) over run (x axis). This is just a matter of finding two points on the y axis and two points on the x axis. Once these points are found we can use our formula to find the slope.

$$\text{(slope)} \ \mathbf{m} = \frac{y2 - y1}{x2 - x1}$$

If $y2 = 4$ and $y1 = 2$
If $x2 = 8$ and $x1 = 3$ $\qquad m = \frac{4-2}{8-3} = \frac{2}{5}$

Graphing Linear Equations

Always remember that for any value given to x or y the statement must be true (in this case equal)!

EXAMPLE:

$$y = x + 3$$

If **x** is 2 than **y** must be 5 because: **5 = 2 + 3**

In this example we will give x three values. We will then solve for y. Next we will plot (find) each value and draw a line connecting each point on the graph. We will keep our equation:

$$y = x + 3.$$

x Values: **Solve for y:**

x = 1   y = 1 + 3   y = 4
x = 2   y = 2 + 3   y = 5
x = 3   y = 3 + 3   y = 6

Next find each set of coordinates: (1, 4); (2, 5); (3, 6)
Remember, the first number is the x axis!

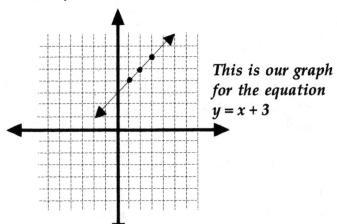

This is our graph for the equation $y = x + 3$

General Math Terms

In this section you will find terms used in several different areas of math.

General Math Terms

Absolute Value

The distance a number is from zero. For example, -7 and +7 have an absolute value of 7. Both -7 and +7 are 7 units away from zero. Written as |7| in a mathematical sentence.

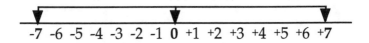

$$-7 \quad -6 \quad -5 \quad -4 \quad -3 \quad -2 \quad -1 \quad \mathbf{0} \quad +1 \quad +2 \quad +3 \quad +4 \quad +5 \quad +6 \quad +\mathbf{7}$$

Average

The sum (total) of a group of numbers added together then divided by the number of addends in that group. **Example:** The average of the numbers 25, 60, and 35 is found as follows:

Add
$$
\begin{array}{r}
25 \\
60 \\
+\ 35 \\
\hline
120
\end{array}
$$
— *3* addends
← sum

Divide

addends ⟶ $3\overline{)120}$ ← *sum*

40 ← our average

$$
\begin{array}{r}
-\underline{120} \\
0
\end{array}
$$

40 is the average

Another Example:

$$25 + 17 + 18 = 60$$

$$60 \div 3 = \mathbf{20} \ \textit{(our average)}$$

153

Algebra

In simple terms it is the process of finding a value of an unknown quantity that uses variables.

EXAMPLE:

In the equation:
$$3x + 2 = 8$$

We must find the value of the variable **x** (unknown) so that 3**x** + 2 is equal to 8. Remember, in algebra, what we do to one side of the equal sign we have to do to the other! Here is how we isolate *x* on one side of the equal sign to find its value:

First, subtract **2** from each side of the equation because it will simplify the problem.

$$3x + 2 = 8 \qquad \underline{\text{From } 3x + 2 = 8 \text{ to}}$$
$$\underline{-2 \quad -2}$$

Now we have $\qquad 3x = 6$

Divide each side of the equal sign by 3

$$\frac{3x}{3} = \frac{6}{3}$$

The 3 in the numerator and denominator cancel each other out
$$\frac{\cancel{3}x}{\cancel{3}} = \frac{6}{3}$$

$$x = \frac{6}{3} = 2$$

We have now solved the mystery of the value for x!

$$\mathbf{x = 2}$$

Capacity

The amount a container will hold.

EXAMPLE: quart, pint, cup, ounce, etc.

Composite Number

All whole numbers that have more factors than one and itself.

EXAMPLE: 4, 6, 8, 9, 10, 12, 14, 15

These are composite numbers because they have more than two factors.

Estimating

A faster way to find an answer when exact values are not needed. This is different from rounding because we round to the **largest** place value and **not** a **given** (specific) place value! Words like *about, around, almost, approximately* identify an estimation.

EXAMPLE:	426
This is exact	+ 296
	722

↓

Now estimate	**4**26	Find the highest place value.
	+ **2**96	We have at least 600!

↓

4**2**6	However, we must look at the next place
+ 2**9**6	value to determine a true estimate.

426 is closer to..........	400
and 296 is closer to...	+ 300
so our estimate is.........	700

155

Another   Example:

$$1,250 \longrightarrow 1,000$$
$$+2,789 \longrightarrow +3,000$$
$$\overline{4,039 \longrightarrow 4000}$$

Expanded Notation

Naming the place value of each digit. For example, the number 122,685 is written in expanded notation this way:

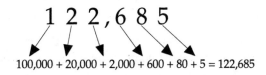

$$100,000 + 20,000 + 2,000 + 600 + 80 + 5 = 122,685$$

Exponents

Shows the number of times the base number is multiplied by itself and an easier way to express larger numbers.

EXAMPLE:

$$3 \times 3 \times 3 \times 3 = 3^4 = 81$$

base number $\longrightarrow 3^4 \longleftarrow$ exponent

so $3 \times 3 \times 3 \times 3 = 3^4 = 3$ to the fourth power

Another way to look at it!

$$\mathbf{3} \times \mathbf{3} = 9$$
$$9 \times \mathbf{3} = 27$$
$$27 \times \mathbf{3} = 81$$

*Notice the **4** threes!*

Greater than

The *greater than* sign is used to identify one number as the larger of two numbers. For example, the problem that 25 is *greater than* 10 can be written as follows:

$$25 > 10$$

The *less than* sign is used to identify one number as the smaller of two numbers. For example, 10 is *less than* 25 can be written as follows:

$$10 < 25$$

Remember, the first number (left to right) is always our point of reference or starting point.

Integers (also see *Multiplying*)

All positive and negative whole numbers including zero.

EXAMPLE: -4, -3, -2, -1, 0, 1, 2, 3, 4 *are all integers.*

Adding & Subtracting

An easy way to remember how to add or subtract integers is to use a number line. Find the <u>first number</u> in the problem then follow the appropriate rule:

When we add a positive we move to the right on the number line.

EXAMPLE: $2 + 3 = {}^+5$

Find **+2** on the line then <u>add</u> **3** (move right):

+2 +3 +4 +5 +6 +7 +8 +9

When we subtract a positive we move to the left on the number line.

EXAMPLE: 5 - (⁺3) = ⁺2

Find **⁺5** on the line then <u>subtract</u> **3** (move left):

When we add a negative we move to the left on the number line.

EXAMPLE: 5 + (⁻3) = ⁺2

Find **⁺5** on the line then <u>subtract</u> **3** (move left):

When we subtract a negative we move to the right on the number line.

EXAMPLE: 2 - (⁻3) = ⁺5

Find **⁺2** on the line then <u>add</u> **3** (move right):

Always start with the first number (positive or negative) in the problem and find it on the number line. Then add or subtract (move left or right) on the number line.

Least Common Multiple (LCM)

Is the lowest number that a group of numbers can divide into (without a remainder). For example, the lowest number (or LCM) that both 3 and 4 can go into is 12. Here is how we came to this conclusion:

Here are multiples of 3   3, 6, 9, **12**, 15, 18, 21, 24.....

Here are multiples of 4   4, 8, **12**, 16, 20, 24, 28......

The **LCM** for 3 and 4 is **12**.

Mixed Numbers

A number that contains both a whole number and a fraction.

EXAMPLE: 2 2/3 is a mixed number.

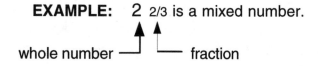

whole number ⎯⎺⎯   ⎯⎺⎯ fraction

Mean

The **average** of a given group of numbers. For example, the mean of the numbers 5, 4, 9, 2 is 5 because:

$$5 + 4 + 9 + 2 = 20$$

$$20 \div 4 = 5$$

$$\begin{array}{r} 5 \\ 4\overline{)20} \end{array} \leftarrow \text{Mean}$$

Median

The middle number in a given set of numbers.

EXAMPLE:

In the set   1, 2, 3, 4, 5, 6, 7, 8, 9

The median or the middle number in the set is 5.

Measurements

(standard)   **(metric)**

The standard unit of measure:

for the UNITED STATES   THE REST OF THE WORLD

12 inches = 1 foot   1 meter = 10 decimeters

3 feet = 1 yard   1 meter = 100 centimeters

1760 yards = 1 mile   1 meter = 1,000 millimeters

5280 feet = 1 mile   1 kilometer = 1,000 meters

                                1 kilometer = 10,000 decimeters

8 ounces = 1 cup   1 kilometer = 100,000 centimeters

2 cups = 1 pint   1 kilometer = 1,000,000 millimeters

2 pints = 1 quart

4 quarts = 1 gallon   *As you can see this unit of*
                              measure is based on multiplying
                              or dividing by 10, 100, or 1,000
                              much like our monitory system.

Mode

Is the number or data that occurs most often.

In the numbers: 2, 3, **5**, 6, 9, 8 , **5**

The mode is **5** because it occurs most often.

Money

A great way to introduce many aspects of math.

EXAMPLES:

$.01 = 1/10 of a dime = 1/100 of a dollar
It takes 100 pennies to make a dollar

$.05 = 1/2 of a dime = 1/20 of a dollar
It takes 20 nickels to make a dollar

$.10 = 1/10 of a dollar
It takes 10 dimes to make a dollar

$.25 = 1/4 of a dollar
It takes 4 quarters to make a dollar

If you'll notice the denominator is how many we need to make one whole.

100 pennies make a dollar	**/100**
20 nickels make a dollar	**/20**
10 dimes make a dollar	**/10**
4 quarters make a dollar	**/4**

Number Line

Helps in visualizing addition and subtraction problems.

$$^-4 \quad ^-3 \quad ^-2 \quad ^-1 \quad 0 \quad ^+1 \quad ^+2 \quad ^+3 \quad ^+4$$

Order of Operation

Here are the rules for doing problems with more than one math function. Do parentheses, exponents & roots, multiplication & division, addition & subtraction in that order!

1. Do parentheses $(3+4) \times 2^2 = 28$

2. Exponents and roots $2^2 \times 4 = 16$

3. Multiplication or Division (from left to right) $3 + 4 \underline{\times} 2 = 11$

4. Addition or Subtraction (from left to right) $4 \underline{+} 2 \underline{-} 3 = 3$

161

Place Value

In a number each digit has a different value. In the number 1,573:

$$\text{The digit } 1 = 1,000$$
$$\text{The digit } 5 = 500$$
$$\text{The digit } 7 = 70$$
$$\text{The digit } 3 = 3$$

Values

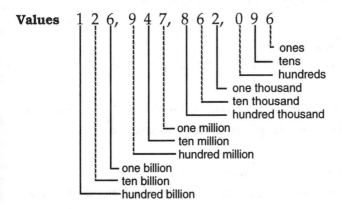

Hint: In the number 2,222 each 2 has a different value. Because the <u>value</u> of a digit depends on the <u>place</u>. Use money as an example. Which digit holds the highest value in the number $202? The two in the hundreds place or the two in the ones place?

Powers of 10

Is a faster way to express very large numbers with 10 as the base number (see exponents). Notice that the exponent (4) also gives us the number of zeros in the final answer.

EXAMPLE:

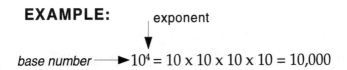

162

Prime Numbers

Are those numbers that have only two factors (1 and itself). For example, 5 is a prime number because the only way to get a product **(using only whole numbers in a multiplication problem)** of 5 is to multiple 1 x 5 = 5. As the definition states, a prime number only has two factors, 1 and itself. The number 4 has 1, 2, and 4 as factors so it is <u>not</u> a prime number, it is a composite number.

Prime Numbers:
2-3-5-7-11-13-17-19-23-29-31-37-41-43-47-53-59-61-67-73-79

Notice that all prime numbers are odd numbers with the exception of the number 2.

Prime Factorization

Is when you factor (take out) only prime numbers out of a given composite number (non prime). For example, 30 can be expressed in a math sentence as:

$$2 \times 15 = \mathbf{30} \longleftarrow composite\ number$$

However, this is not prime factorization because 15 is not a prime number. To use prime factorization we must use <u>only</u> prime numbers as factors. What prime numbers can we use to factor out of 15? How about 3 & 5? Here is how we use prime factorization for the number 30.

$$2 \times \underline{\mathbf{15}} = 30$$

Is now expressed: $2 \times (\mathbf{3 \times 5}) = 30$

Prime numbers are 2, 3, and 5. <u>*This is prime factorization*</u>.

163

Probability

The likelihood that something will occur. This is written as:

PROBABILITY $= \dfrac{\text{number of favorable outcomes}}{\text{number of possible outcomes}}$

EXAMPLE:

If we roll a die once there is a one in six (1/6 or 1:6) chance that we will roll a 5. This is because there are six numbers on a die and only one is the number 5.

Proportions

Two equivalent ratios. Say two out of four children like pizza. This means that for every four children, two will like pizza. This can be reduced to lower terms and we could say for every two children one will like pizza.

EXAMPLE: Written as a fraction:

$$\frac{2}{4} = \frac{1}{2}$$

EXAMPLE: Written as a ratio:

$$2:4 = 1:2$$

For every four kids two will like pizza, for every two kids one will like pizza, and so on.

Pythagorean Theorem

In any right triangle with sides *a* and *b* and hypotenuse side *c*. For example:

$$a^2 + b^2 = c^2$$

$a = 3$
$b = 4$
$c = ????????$

Using the formula $a^2 + b^2 = c^2$ we can find the answer.

$$a^2 + b^2 = c^2$$

$$3^2 + 4^2 = c^2$$

$$9 + 16 = c^2$$

$$25 = c^2$$

Now we know that c^2 is 25. What is **c**? Find the square root of 25 and you will have solved the value of c.

$$\sqrt{25} = \sqrt{c^2} = \sqrt{5^2}$$

the $\sqrt{5^2}$ is........ 5

Range

From the lowest (fewest) to the highest (most) in a set of numbers.

EXAMPLE:

In the set of numbers:

$$5, 10, 25, 79, 81, 82$$

The range is **77** because counting from 5 to 82 equals 77.

We can just subtract the smallest number from the largest number:

$$82 - 5 = \mathbf{77}$$

So, once again, the range is **77**.

Rational Numbers

Any positive or negative number. Numbers can be:

composites (2, 4, 6, 8)
primes (2, 3, 5, 7)
fractions (2/4)
improper fractions (4/3)
mixed numbers (3 3/4)
variables (x)
integers (⁻4 or +4), etc.

Ratios

Is a comparison of two numbers by division. For example, the ratio of 1 to 5 can be written as a fraction 1/5 or as a ratio 1:5. This means one out of every 5.

Reciprocal

Two numbers that are multiplied together and their product is equal to 1.

EXAMPLE:

$$\frac{3}{4} \times \frac{4}{3} = \frac{12}{12} \text{ or } 1$$

3/4 and 4/3 are reciprocals

Another way of looking at reciprocals is just inverting the fraction (turning upside down).

Roman Numerals

Are numbers that are represented by letters. Although their usage has diminished over the years they are still used in outlining, older movies, and the Superbowl.

EXAMPLES:

I = 1   V = 5   X = 10   L = 50
C = 100   D = 500   M = 1000

Here is the difficult aspect of this numbering system. How do we write numbers such as 4? When a smaller value symbol is before (left to right) a larger symbol we subtract the value of the smaller symbol.

EXAMPLE: IV = 4 (5-1)

I is smaller then V so we subtract one from five.

Others:

IX = 9 (10-1)   CM = 900 (1,000-100)
IL = 49 (50-1)   IC = 99 (100-1)

Smaller symbols in front of larger symbols we add.

EXAMPLE:

VI = 6 (5+1)
XI = 11 (10+1)
LX = 60 (50+10)
MCX = 1,110 (1,000+100+10)

Rounding

Is similar to estimating because we round numbers to make it easier to calculate an answer. The key is to know what number we want to round. **EXAMPLE:** We want to round the number 1,573 to the nearest tens place value. Follow the rules to make it simpler.

Rules

1. Identify the digit (place value) we want to round: ***tens***

1,5$\overline{7}$3

In this case we want to round to the tens place value.

2. Look at the digit immediately to the right of the 7, we find it is the digit 3 (1,57**3**).

3. If the 3 were **five** or larger, the 7 should change to an eight. However, if the digit is **four** or less the 7 should remain a 7. In this case the 7 will remain a 7.

4. After we round to the tens place we change all the smaller digits to zero (157**0**).

5. Now the number has changed from 1,573 to 1,570. We rounded to the nearest tens place value.

Lets round to the nearest 10,000 place value:

Identify place value:	1,5<u>6</u>7,543
Look at the number to the right:	1,56<u>7</u>,543
7 is larger than 4 so we round up to:	1,57
6 rounds to 7 and all the other smaller place values turn to zero:	1,57<u>0,000</u>

from 1,567,543 *to* 1,570,000

Hint: Tell your kids to identify the place value to be rounded and then the number to the right. Often times kids look at large numbers and they are overwhelmed. They only need to worry about two place values (two digits)!

Scale

Drawing items smaller than their original form but drawing everything with the same (fixed) proportions. This is used when drawing items larger than the paper being used, such as maps and buildings.

EXAMPLE:

This could be the scale drawing of a football field where every inch equals 3,600 inches or 1:3,600 scale.

1 inch = 100 yards
1 inch = 3,600 inches

Scientific Notation

A faster way to show mathematical expressions using exponents. For example, a normal multiplication sentence can look like this:

$$6 \times 1{,}000 = 6{,}000$$

Using scientific notation, the same math sentence looks like this: Notice the exponent equals the number of zeros!

$$6 \times 10^3 = 6{,}000$$

The decimal point moves to the right when there is a positive exponent:

$$6.2195 \times 10^4 = 62{,}195.0$$

With positive exponents (10^4) the decimal point moves to the right **4** places to make the number larger. Now look at the same problem using a negative exponent:

$$62{,}195.0 \times 10^{-4} = 6.2\,1\,9\,5\,0$$

end here   4 3 2 1   **start here**

With a negative exponent the decimal point is moved to the left
4 places to make the number smaller. If there are no more digits on the left add zeros to make the number correct.

$$57 \times 10^{-4} = .0\,0\,5\,7$$

$$.0\,0\,5\,7.$$

to here   **from here**

Move to the left **4** decimal places making it smaller.

Square

When a number is multiplied by itself the number is said to be squared. All of the following mean the same thing:

EXAMPLE:

$$4 \times 4 = 16$$
$$4^2 = 16$$

4 squared is 16

16 is the square of 4

and 4 is the square root of 16

Square Root

A square root is a product of a number multiplied by itself.

EXAMPLES:

$4 \times 4 = 4^2 = 16$ The square root of 16 is **4** ($\sqrt{16} = 4$)

$5 \times 5 = 5^2 = 25$ The square root of 25 is **5** ($\sqrt{25} = 5$)

$6 \times 6 = 6^2 = 36$ The square root of 36 is **6** ($\sqrt{36} = 6$)

$7 \times 7 = 7^2 = 49$ The square root of 49 is **7** ($\sqrt{49} = 7$)

Temperature Converting

	freezing	*boiling*
Fahrenheit	32°	212°
Centigrade	0	100

How to convert:

Fahrenheit to Centigrade:

$$\frac{5(F-32)}{9}$$

Centigrade to Fahrenheit:

$$\frac{(C \times 9)}{5} + 32$$

Time

If your children are just learning to tell time it may be easier to start with a digital clock. You can use television listings to help them understand the concept of the hour and half hour. As they advance this would be a good way to introduce fractions such as 1/2 and 1/4.

1/2 past the hour   1/4 past the hour

Variables

A symbol that stands for a number. This symbol is usually a letter.

$$3\underline{n} + 2 = 8$$

Variable Expression

Is an expression that contains at least one variable.

EXAMPLE:

$$3n + 2 = 8$$

n is the variable in this equation

Weights (see Measurements)

Greatest Common Factor (GCF)

The largest number that can be factored into any given set of numbers. For example, the numbers 10 & 15 have a GCF of 5 because 5 is the largest common factor of 10 & 15. This is a simple problem. However, most of the time it is necessary to find several factors in a given set of numbers before determining the *GCF*. For example, what is the *GCF* of 48 and 72? First, find all the factors of 48 & 72.

48 has the following factors:

1, 2, 3, 4, 6, 8, 12, 16, **24**, 48

72 has the following factors:

1, 2, 3, 4, 6, 8, 9, 12, 18, **24**, 36, 72

What is the largest factor (GCF) of both numbers? The answer is **24**.

Another EXAMPLE:

44 has the following factors: 1, 2, **4**, 11, 22, 44

40 has the following factors: 1, 2, **4**, 5, 8, 10, 20, 40

What is the **GCF** of 44 and 40? The answer is **4**.

Solving Word Problems

Most learners have difficulty solving word problems because they **do not** know how to identify the important information. Just like every other part of this book we only look at one small portion of information or data at a time!

Here we go.....

1) Make a list of all numbers in the problem.

2) Identify what type of answer is required by viewing key words in the problem. *See key words below*

Key Words

Addition	Subtraction	Multiplication	Division
all together	difference	all groups	in each
in all	remain	product	separate
total	left	by	each group
together	less	times	split
sum	change	of	
both/all	fewer		

3) Cross out all unimportant information so not to confuse the learner.

4) Put all the important numbers in a mathematical expression.

EXAMPLE:

Dan and **Mandy** went to Disneyland for the 4th of July. At the end of the day they **split** the remaining **$12.50**. How much did Mandy have to spend for dinner on the trip home?

Key Words

2 *(people)*
split *(division)*
$12.50

Math Expression

$12.50 ÷ 2 =

Science

Science

Absolute Zero

It is the coldest possible temperature when all molecule motion stops. If we look at solids, liquids, and gases we know that they are determined by molecule motion or the lack of motion. The absolute zero thus determined is -273.15 deg C (-459.67 deg F). This temperature is the zero point of the absolute Kelvin degree and Rankine temperature scales. The fact that absolute zero is unattainable in any real process is known as the *Third Law of Thermodynamics*.

Acceleration

It is the change of speed of a given object. This is measured in units of velocity such as feet per second or mph. The concepts of "speeding up" and "slowing down" actually imply positive and negative accelerations (negative acceleration is commonly called deceleration). For example, if the speed of an automobile traveling in a straight line increases from 15 to 25 meters per second (34 to 55 mph) in 10 seconds, then the auto's average acceleration is 1 m/sec per second (2.1 mph per second). The auto's speed increases every second by an amount equal to 1 m/sec.

Acetylsalicylic Acid

This is our common aspirin.

Acids

Originally recognized by its sour taste in water. In chemistry terms acids are electron acceptors, proton donors, and capable of yielding hydrogen ions.

Amino Acids

Organic compounds that are the building blocks of proteins. In most animal metabolisms, a number of amino acids play an essential role. The *genitic code*, which determines the assembly of amino acids into body proteins, is mediated by the nucleic acids. Amino acids join together in long chains, the amino group of one amino acid linking with the carboxyl group of another. The linkage is known as a peptide bond, and a chain of amino acids is known as a polypeptide. Proteins are large, naturally-occurring polypeptides. Many different amino acids are found, about 20 of which are the main constituents of proteins. Only about half of these are classified as essential nutrients, that is, necessary in the human diet.

Anatomy

The part of biology involving the structure of plants, animals, and other forms of biological organisms. Anatomy is divided into several subdisciplines. Gross anatomy involves studies on structures that can be seen with the naked eye. Histology is the study of tissue structure and cytology that of cell structure. Histological and cytological studies require the use of a microscope, they are known together as microscopic anatomy. When the word functional is placed before any of these words, as in "functional anatomy," reference is being made to the subject of physiology. Often anatomy cannot be discussed properly without introducing some physiology, and physiology can almost never be discussed properly without an anatomical background.

Animal Products

Those products made directly and indirectly from animals. An example, a direct product would be the meat we eat and an example of an indirect product would be those products that are made with the help of animal products such as a baseball glove is made from cowhide.

Asteroids

Rocks orbiting in the **asteroid belt** located between Mars and Jupiter. There are some 75 Amor asteroids (whose orbits intersect the orbit of Mars), 50 Apollo asteroids (whose orbits intersect the Earth's orbit), and 16 Trojan asteroids (which precede or follow Jupiter in its orbit in gravitationally bound positions that form equilateral triangles with Jupiter and the Sun). Asteroids continue to be discovered.

Science

One Apollo asteroid, previously unknown, passed within 800,000 km (500,000 mi) of Earth in 1989--the closest approach of a large asteroid since that of Hermes in 1937. However, there have been others such as the undetected asteroids that "sneak up" on Earth.

Atmospheric Layers

Different layers of gases that surround the earth. Nitrogen makes up 78% of the atmosphere while oxygen (21%) and trace gases make up the rest. There are four layers of the atmosphere starting with the closest to the ground called the Troposphere, then the Stratosphere, Mesosphere, and the Thermosphere. Each has a different temperature range. Temperatures decrease with altitude in the troposphere and mesosphere and increase with altitude in the stratosphere and thermosphere.

Atoms

The smallest unit of measure that is recognized as a chemical element. Atoms of different elements may also combine into systems called **molecules**, the smallest units of chemical compounds. The size of a typical atom is only about 10^{-10} meters. Atoms cannot be seen using optical microscopes, because they are much smaller than the wavelengths of visible light. By using more advanced imaging techniques such as electron microscopes scientists have been able to produce images in which the sites of individual atoms can be identified.

Bases

Substances that are usually soapy to the touch and that could react with acids in water to make salts. Also capable of combining with a proton to form a new substance.

Biosphere

The part (region) of the earth that can support and sustain life. This includes the atmosphere, water, and soil. Its unique properties make it possible for the continuing evolution of life forms.

Science

Carbohydrates

Include cellulose, starches, sugars, and other compounds are the most common single class of organic substances found in nature. This is a major nutritional source needed by animals for energy.

Carbon Dating

Radiometric age-dating, or radiometric dating, is the determination of the age of materials by means of their radioactive contents.

Carbon Dioxide

A colorless, odorless, incombustible gas that is exhaled from animals, taken in by plants as fuel, and given off when fuel is burned. It has one atom of carbon and two atoms of oxygen. Also used in food refrigeration, carbonated beverages, fire extinguishers, and aerosols.

Carboniferous Period

A geological period noted for its lush plant growth about 290 to 350 million years ago. At that time the equator went through North America and Europe.

Carbon Monoxide

A colorless, odorless, highly poisonous gas formed by the incomplete combustion of carbon or a carboneous material such as gasoline.

Cardiovascular

Pertaining to the heart and circulatory system. The circulatory system consists of two interconnected systems, both originating in the heart. The systemic circulation and the pulmonary circulation. In the systemic, or greater, circulation, blood is pumped from the left ventricle of the heart into the **aorta**. It is then distributed by a series of increasingly smaller arteries into the tiny capillaries in which the blood circulates through the body tissues. From

Science

the capillaries in the tissues the blood is then collected in veins of increasing diameter, finally entering the right atrium of the heart.

Carnivore

An animal that eats animal flesh. A true carnivore consumes only animal flesh and little else. A good example would be the tyrannosaurus rex or our current day wolf.

Cell

The smallest unit of an organism capable of independent function.

Characteristics, Inherited

Personal characteristics we get directly from our parents. An example of this would be the color of our eyes or hair.

Chloride

Compound of an element with chlorine. Examples include sodium chloride (table salt) and potassium chloride (salt substitute).

Cholesterol

A waxy complex substance found in animal tissue. It is manufactured by the body. It is important in nerve functions and hormone production. Cholesterol level is the amount of cholesterol in the blood given in milligrams per 100 milliliters (mg%).

Chromosomes

A strand of DNA associated with proteins in the nucleus of animal and plant cells that carry the genes and function in the transmission of hereditary information.

Circuit

A closed path capable of carrying an electric current. Contains a configuration of components designed for specific uses.

Science

Clouds

Cumulonimbus clouds are tall dark cumulus clouds or thunderheads. Cumulus clouds are white fluffy clouds that resemble cotton. When clouds form at ground surface they are called fog. Clouds that form in the middle troposphere are called altostratus and altocumulus, and those in the upper troposphere are referred to as cirrocumulus, cirrostratus, or cirrus. For those with bases in the lower troposphere, the terms stratus and cummulus are used. When precipitation is falling from these clouds, they are referred to with such terms as nimbostratus or cumulonimbus. Nimbostratus are the gray, leaden-sky clouds often produced by large-scale winter cyclones in which precipitation is fairly steady and long-lasting. Cumulonimbus clouds, on the other hand, are associated with typical summertime thunderstorms, in which rainfall is generally brief but heavy.

Comet

Consists chiefly of ammonia, methane, carbon dioxide, and water. All comet orbits that have been established are elliptical. Short-period comets have periods of less than 200 years and their orbits are mostly inclined at a small angle to the orbital plane of the Earth (the ecliptic). The comet with the shortest known period is Encke's comet (3.3 years). Long-period comets have periods of more than 200 years. About 100 of each group of periodic comets are known, and 800 nonperiodic comets have been observed.

Compounds, Chemical

A substance in which two or more elements are joined by chemical bonds. Compounds usually have unique properties unlike those of their constituent elements. A compound can be created or broken down by means of a chemical reation but not by mechanical or physical separation techniques, such as chromatography. A compound's smallest unit is a molecule, a molecule, however, is not necessarily a compound but sometimes consists of atoms of the same element. A molecule of water for instance, is a compound, but one of oxygen gas is not.

Condense
To change from a gas to a liquid.

Convection Currents
The circular movement of gases or liquids that result in differences of temperature.

Digestion
To convert food into simpler chemical compounds that can be absorbed by the body. This is done in several parts of the body beginning in the mouth and ending in the intestine.

DNA Deoxyribonucleic Acid, and ribonucleic acid (RNA)
Are the two chemical substances involved in the genetic transmission of characteristics from parent to offspring and in the manufacture of proteins.

Doppler Radar
Radar that shows distance and direction of movement of an object. Often used to show the movement of cloud formations and now is used by meteorologists to show weather patterns.

Earthquakes
A shifting or movement of the Earth's crust. An earthquake is the shaking or trembling of the crust of the earth caused by volcanic forces or by the shifting of rock beneath the surface. In the recent years considerable progress has been made toward predicting earthquakes. However, there are general predictions and precise predictions of earthquakes do not exist at this time. The actual movement of the earth is seldom the direct cause of death or injury. However, the shifting of the ground causes buildings and other structures to shake or collapse. Most casualties result from falling objects, debris, glass, and fire.

Science

Eclipse, Solar
When the moon moves directly in between the sun and earth.

Eclipse, Lunar
When the earth is between the moon and sun.

Electricity
Electricity is a form of energy, a phenomenon that is a result of the existence of electrical charge. The theory of electricity and its inseparable effect, magnetism, is probably the most accurate and complete of all scientific theories. The understanding of electricity has led to the invention of motors, generators, telephones, radio and television, X-ray devices, computers, and nuclear energy systems.

Elements
Are samples of matter that cannot be separated into a simpler unit by chemical or physical means. There are 109 know elements. These elements are categorized on the periodic table by their atomic weight. Hydrogen and helium are first and second on the table.

Endangered
Endangered species are those whose populations have been so reduced that they are threatened with extinction. Thousands of species are included in this category. The International Union for the Conservation of Nature and Natural Resources publishes a list of threatened mammals, birds, reptiles, and amphibians.

Endocrine System
This system consists of specialized glands located in different parts of the body that adjust the activities of the body to the changing demands of the external and internal environment.

Science

Energy

Energy is the capacity for doing work. Energy can be measured in terms of mechanical work, but because not all forms of energy can be converted into useful work, it is more precise to say that the energy of a system changes by an amount equal to the net work done on the system. In classical physics, energy, like work, is considered a scalar quantity and the units of energy are the same as those of work. These units may be ergs, joules, watt-hours, foot-pounds, or foot-pounds, depending on the system of units being used.

FORMS OF ENERGY

Energy exists in many different forms. The form that bodies in motion possess is called kinetic energy. Energy may be stored in the form of potential energy, as in a compressed spring. Chemical systems possess internal energy, which can be converted by various devices into useful work. For example, a fuel such as gasoline can be burned in an engine to propel a vehicle. Heat energy may be absorbed or released when the internal energy of a system changes while work is done on or by the system.

Mass and Energy

Einstein first established that mass itself is one form of energy; this is indicated by the well-known relation $E = mc^2$, which may be interpreted to mean that if a mass m can be converted into energy, the amount of energy produced is given by the product of the mass and the square of the speed of light, c. Because the speed of light is a large number (c = 3 X 10 billion cm/sec), an enormous amount of energy is contained in ordinary matter, but it is generally impractical to convert this mass into useful energy.

Kinetic Energy

Masses in motion possess kinetic energy. For instance, an object of mass m moving with speed v possesses kinetic

Science

energy one-half mv². A wheel with a moment of inertia, spinning about its center of mass with a variable angular speed represented by the Greek letter omega, has a kinetic energy equal to one-half the moment of inertia times the square of the angular speed. If either of these objects could be brought to rest by appropriate means, useful work could be done. For example, a pulley and rope attached to the wheel could be made to lift a weight. When the speed of an object becomes comparable to the speed of light, such expressions for kinetic energy are no longer valid and must be modified according to the *Theory of Relativity*.

Potential Energy

A compressed spring possesses energy that can be converted to work by allowing the spring to exert a force against an external device and to move until the spring assumes its original length. When a mass of weight W is lifted to a height h, the mass possesses gravitational potential energy Wh, which can be regained by lowering the mass. Electrical charges possess electrostatic potential energy, which can be converted to work by allowing the charges to move toward or away from each other.

Internal Energy

Energy contained in a system by virtue of the motions and forces between the individual atoms and molecules of the system. When the internal energy of a body changes, heat energy is sometimes generated or absorbed. For instance, if a piece of metal is placed in a flame, the temperature of the metal will rise, heat has been absorbed by the metal and its internal energy has been increased thus the atoms of the metal are vibrating more rapidly and may be at different distances from one another.

Mechanical Equivalent of Heat

The relationship between heat energy, which is usually measured by observing temperature changes in an object, and mechanical work is called the mechanical equivalent of

Science

heat. The relationship is expressed as follows: 1 calorie = 4.186 joules, where 1 calorie is the heat required to raise the temperature of 1 deg gm of water 1 deg C.

Enzyme
A substance especially important to digestion. Various enzymes in the stomach and intestines breakdown proteins, carbohydrates, and fats so that they are easily absorbed.

Eon
An extremely long period of time that could be as long as one million years.

Epicenter
The origination point of an earthquake.

Erosion
Is the wearing down of rock by natural forces. Nature uses gravity, ice, ocean waves, wind, and running water to change the rock. See weathering

Excretory System
Special structures in through which waste products of metabolism are rid and the proper balance of water and salts in the blood and other body fluids are maintained at the same levels.

Extinct
When a species no longer exists.

Fats (and acids)
A diverse class of animal and vegetable compounds used extensively as foods, cleansers, and lubricants.

Flight
Flight is the ability to move with direction through the air, an ability shared by many animals. Humans can fly only in the

Science

machines they have devised. Bats, most birds, and many insects practice true natural flight: that is, the motions of their wings produce the air lift necessary to take off, fly, and land. A number of other kinds of animals can glide for brief distances through the air. They do so by means of stretchable body membranes, as with various small mammals and some lizards and snakes, or by means of enlarged fins, such as the flying fish. A few species of fish actually flap their fins in the air like birds.

Food Chain
The path that nutrients take in a certain ecosystem.

Force
The amount of push or pull used against an object.

Friction The rubbing together of two objects. The more resistance an object has the more force that is required to move over the object which also means the more friction created.

Lubrication A substance that reduces the amount of friction between objects.

Resistance Is something that stops or prevents an object from moving. In order for an object to be moved the force has to be greater than the resistance. Try rubbing a cotton ball over a piece of sandpaper and then over the kitchen table. There is a large difference in resistance!

Fossil
A plant or animal that has been preserved, somewhat, and is often found in sedimentary rock. Preserved by burial under countless layers of sedimentary material, fossils are a record of the history of life beginning approximately 3.5 billion years ago, the study of which is called paleontology.

Science

Friction

The universal force between surfaces that oppose sliding motion. When surfaces of two bodies are in contact, the interactive force at the surface may have components both perpendicular and tangent to the surface. The perpendicular component is called the normal force, and the tangential component is called the friction force. If there is relative sliding at the surface, the friction force always acts in the opposite direction of this motion.

Galvanizing

A process where iron or steel is plated with zinc. This process helps prevent rust forming when the metal must be exposed to the elements. Electroplating is the deposition of a metal onto a metallic surface from a solution by electrolysis. It is used for purposes of decoration and protection of the metal. Metals commonly used to plate surfaces are silver, nickel, chromium, cadmium, zinc, gold, and copper. In the case of copper plating, for example, electroplating takes place by means of the reaction in which a copper ion is carried to the metal surface to be plated, known as the cathode, from the source of the metal being plated, known as the anode. The ion is forced to the cathode by an external source such as a battery. The electrolytic solution is a salt of the metal being plated; in the case of copper plating, it is copper sulfate. The appearance, adhesion, porosity, and protection value of electroplated coatings depend on several things, including the type of base metal to be plated, the preparation of the metal for plating, and the electrode position process itself.

Gravity

The force that attracts all objects in the universe.

Greenhouse Effect

The trapping of heat by the air surrounding the earth. In environmental science, the greenhouse effect is a popular term for the role that carbon dioxide, water vapor, and

Science

trace gases play in keeping the Earth's surface warmer than it would be without their presence. The atmosphere, when clear, is nearly transparent to the primarily shortwave radiation from the Sun, most of which is absorbed at the Earth's surface. The Earth, being much cooler than the Sun, remits radiation most strongly at shortwave (infrared) wavelengths. The atmosphere's carbon dioxide, water vapor, and trace gases then absorb much of this radiation and remit a large proportion of it back toward the Earth. The atmosphere thus acts as a kind of blanket (although one with holes in it), without its presence, the Earth's average ground temperature of 15 deg C (60 deg F) would fall to -28 deg C (-20 deg F). The term greenhouse effect implies that a comparable effect keeps the interior of a greenhouse warm. Actually, the main role of the glass in a greenhouse, besides that of admitting solar radiation, is to prevent convection currents from mixing cooler air outside with the warm air inside.

Habitats

Where a particular species lives. Fish live in water, man lives on land, etc. A habitat is the place where a particular animal or plant species dwells. Habitats of similar climate and vegetation form land complexes called *biomes*. The natural habitats on Earth and the great variety of species are a product of the changes that have occurred over long geological time periods, however, not all habitats are natural. Humans can alter nature and thereby promote the welfare of certain species that would otherwise not occur in the same numbers. Some ecologists consider an organism's total physical and chemical surroundings (the environment) synonymous with habitat. No description of habitat is complete without including some environmental parameters such as temperature and dissolved oxygen.

Herbivore

Herbivores are organisms that eat chiefly plant rather than animal materials. All herbivorous mammals have characteristic adaptations, such as their teeth are commonly specialized to accommodate a plant diet, their digestive system is longer and more complicated than that of carnivores because it is more difficult to digest vegetation than meat.

High Pressure

An area where cool air sinks and pushes down to the ground with increased pressure. A high-pressure region, area, or cell is a portion of the atmosphere in which a column of air has more gas molecules than a comparable column elsewhere and hence exerts a greater pressure at the Earth's surface. Because air in the central portions is sinking, such a region has fair, clear weather. High-pressure regions are a few hundred to a few thousand kilometers in diameter. Largest and most persistent are the subtropical anticyclones over the oceans around 30 deg N (Azores or Bermuda High, Hawaiian High) and 30 deg S (in the southern Atlantic, Indian, and eastern Pacific oceans). These form as the descending branches of the hadley cells, from them the trade winds blow toward the equator.

Hydrosphere

The region of water at or near the Earth's surface. It is distinguished from the lithosphere (rocks), the biosphere (living things), and the atmosphere (air). The total volume of water in the hydrosphere is approximately 1.5 billion km(3), 99 percent of which is contained in the continuous waters of the oceans and seas. The remainder is divided among groundwater, glaciers, and ice sheets, freshwater lakes, water vapor, rivers and streams. The Earth's water circulates and interacts in the hydrologic cycles, whereby water falling as rain runs off as rivers into the oceans and evaporates back into the atmosphere.

Science

Invertebrates

The invertebrate group is one of the two general categories of animals. The other group, vertebrates, includes those animals having backbones composed of a series of articulating vertebrae (fishes, amphibians, reptiles, birds, and mammals). Invertebrates lack vertebrae and include the remainder of the animal kingdom. The invertebrate group covers a wide range of organisms, from simple single-celled protozoans to those members of the phylum Chordata that lack a vertebral column. As such it is also an artificial category, splitting the phylum Chordata and including all the other phyla. Thus, invertebrates constitute almost the entire animal kingdom. Still, it is a useful category and unites a diverse assemblage of organisms that may be studied by a common approach distinct from the study of vertebrates.

Light

Light is electromagnetic radiation in the wavelength range extending from about 0.4 micron to about 0.7 micron. Perhaps more properly, the visual response to electromagnetic radiation in this range. By extension, the term is frequently applied to adjacent wavelength ranges that the eye cannot detect, ultraviolet light, infrared light, and black light. In addition to wavelength, frequency, in hertz, and wave number, in inverse units of length, are also used to specify and designate the character and quality of the radiation. Associated with wavelength or frequency is the visual response of color. The term monochromatic is applied to the idealized situation in which the light in a beam is all of one wavelength.

Characteristics of Light

Light is characterized not only by wavelength, essentially a temporal quality, but also by state and degree of polarization, a geometric or directional quality, and by intensity, essentially a physical quality. The visual response to intensity is brightness. In the human visual system, at least, there is no counterpart response, to the state and degree of polarization, but ample evidence exists that certain arthropods, bees in particular, are sensitive to the state of polarization of sky light. There is some speculation that certain migrating birds may also respond to this quality of light.

Lithosphere

The Earth's solid outer shell. The lithosphere is the solid portion of the Earth, in contrast to the atmosphere and the hydrosphere. In a more restricted sense, it is the crust, or outer, rigid shell, of the Earth, as opposed to the mantle and core, which together comprise the barysphere, or centrosphere.

Low Pressure

An area where warm air rises which creates less pressure, or lower pressure, on that given area. A portion of the atmosphere with fewer molecules than adjacent portions is called a low-pressure region, area, or cell, or simply a low. In such a region a column of air exerts less pressure on the Earth's surface than do nearby columns. Because air is generally rising in such systems, they are cloudy, usually rainy, and often stormy. Low-pressure cells may be less than 1 km (0.6 mi) across in a tornado, about 100 km (60 mi) across in a hurricane, or more than 1,000 km (600 mi) across in a mature mid latitude cyclone. The largest are the semipermanent lows around Iceland and the Aleutian Islands, the low-pressure belt encircling Antarctica, and the region (variously called the doldrums, the tropical rainy belt, or the intertropical convergence zone) where the trade winds end in a region of warm, rising air near the equator.

Machines

Simple machines increase our ability and speed to do work. Machines increase the amount of force applied and they change the direction of force applied. There are several

Science

types of simple machines such as: the lever (like a hammer pulling a nail), wheel and axle (just look at your bicycle sprocket), inclined plane pushing a wheelbarrow up a ramp), the pulley, and the wedge.

Magnetism

The force that can repel or draw objects together. These objects are called magnets. Most magnets are made of metals, however, some are made of other materials. The earth is a large magnet with a **magnetic field** surrounding it. Magnetism is caused by electric charges moving within a magnetic material. When an electric charge moves it produces magnetism and when a magnet moves it produces an electrical charge. These forces create the *magnetic field*.

Matter

Matter is any substance that possesses mass and occupies space. Thus, gases, liquids, solids, and plasmas are all different forms of matter. Because electromagnetic radiation is known to possess mass, it may be useful for some purposes to consider radiation also to be a form of matter. Scientific progress has led more and more deeply into an understanding of the structure of matter. During the 19th century the molecular theory of matter was developed, which considered all matter to be composed of tiny, indivisible entities called molecules. The study of chemical reactions led to the discovery of atoms as more fundamental building blocks of matter. Water was found to be a molecule composed of two atoms of hydrogen and one atom of oxygen. The atomic theory of matter holds that all matter is made up of molecules, which in turn are composed of atoms, it was established that approximately a hundred distinct elementary atoms exist that can bind together to form myriad different molecules.

Science

Mesosphere

The warm stratopause, about 0 deg C (32 deg F) in temperature and existing roughly 50 km (30 mi) above sea level, and the cold mesopause, about -90 deg C (-130 deg F) and 80 km (50 mi) above sea level, form the lower and upper boundaries of the mesosphere. The decrease of temperature with increasing altitude has the same physical causes as the temperature decrease within the troposphere: absorption of solar radiation at the base and the adiabatic cooling of rising air parcels.

Metabolism

The sum of all the chemical reactions in the living cell that are used for the production of useful work and the synthesis of cell constituents. Metabolism is the sum of all the chemical reactions in the living cell that are used for the production of useful work and the synthesis of cell constituents. Almost all cellular reactions are catalyzed by complex protein molecules called enzymes, which are capable of speeding reaction rates by a factor of hundreds to millions.

Meteors

Also known as a shooting stars, the streak of light produced by the evaporation of interplanetary particles as they enter the Earth's atmosphere.

Moon

The only natural satellite of the Earth. It has a diameter of 2,160 miles which makes it about one-fourth the size of Earth.

Newton's Third Law of Motion

States that to every action there is an equal and opposite reaction. The law applies to pushing a child on a swing or an airplane propeller pulling and pushing air.

Science

Nucleic Acids
Deoxyribonucleic acid (DNA) and ribonucleic acid (RNA) are the two chemical substances involved in the genetic transmission of characteristics from parent to offspring and in the manufacture of proteins. Throughout the early 20th century, it was known that chromosomes, the genetic material of cells, contain DNA.

Omnivore
Eats both meat and vegetation.

Photosynthesis
Photosynthesis is the biological process by which the energy of sunlight is absorbed and used to power the formation of organic compounds from carbon dioxide and water. Although primarily associated with green plants, photosynthesis also occurs in algae and a limited number of bacteria. This process ultimately supplies the energy required by all living organisms for their continued survival.

Planets
Mercury
3,031 miles in diameter
36,000,000 miles from sun
88 days to orbit the sun

Venus
7,500 miles in diameter
67,000,000 miles from sun
225 days to orbit the sun

Earth
24,902 miles (40,075 km) in circumference
7,926 miles (12,756 km) in diameter
93,000,000 miles from the sun
Takes 24 hours to make one full rotation on its axis
75% is covered with water, 25% with land
Orbit - It takes 365.25 days to orbit the sun

Science

Mars
4,215 miles in diameter
141,500,000 miles from sun
687 days to orbit the sun

Jupiter
88,700 miles in diameter
483,000,000 miles from sun
12 years to orbit the sun

Saturn
75,000 miles in diameter
887,000,000 miles from sun
29.46 years to orbit the sun

Uranus
32,500 miles in diameter
1,780,000,000 miles from sun
84 years to orbit the sun

Neptune
30,700 miles in diameter
2,790,000,000 miles from sun
164.79 years to orbit the sun

Pluto
1,660 miles in diameter
3,500,000,000 miles from sun
247.7 years to orbit the sun

Plants

The energy obtained from food is first converted from sunlight to usable, transferable energy by green plants. The oxygen supply in the Earth's atmosphere is a result of photosynthesis by green plants. Fossil fuels come from plant material. Plants also create and modify local environmental conditions on which many species of animals and other plants depend.

Science

Proteins
Proteins are molecules essential to maintaining the structure and function of all living organisms. Proteins have many different properties and function in a variety of ways. For example, enzymes, hemoglobin, and collagen of bones, tendons, and skin; and certain hormones all are proteins.

Rain Forest
Jungle and rain forest are terms that are often used synonymously but with little precision. The more meaningful and restrictive of these terms is rain forest, which refers to the climax or primary forest in regions with high rainfall (greater than 1.8 m/70 in per year), chiefly but not exclusively found in the tropics. Rain forests are significant for their valuable timber resources, and in the tropics they afford sites for commercial crops such as rubber, tea, coffee, bananas, and sugarcane. They also include some of the last remaining areas of the Earth that are both unexploited economically and inadequately known scientifically.

Respiratory System
An aerobic organism must abstract oxygen from environmental air or water in order to support its life functions. This includes the mouth, nose, trachea (windpipe), and lungs. The process of obtaining oxygen and releasing the cellular waste product, carbon dioxide, into the environment is known as respiration. Multicellular organisms, however, had to evolve specialized respiratory systems for supplying oxygen to their tissues and removing excess carbon dioxide. These systems are capable of functioning over a wide range of metabolic demands and within a minimum energy expenditure.

RNA
See Nucleic Acid

Science

Rock

Rock is the solid substance that forms the Earth's crust. Most geologists exclude soil from this category and further restrict the term to materials formed by natural process. Rocks are classified as igneous, sedimentary, or metamorphic according to how they formed. Those that solidified from molten or partly molten material are called igneous rocks. **Sedimentary** rocks form by the accumulation of sediment, mineral particles that have either settled from a state of suspension in air or water or have been precipitated from a state of solution. **Metamorphic** rocks are those that have undergone marked transformation, in response to heat, pressure, or chemical alteration. The molten material (magma) from which all **igneous** rocks form may issue as lava from volcanoes, such rock is said to be extrusive. Intrusive igneous rocks are those that form from consolidation of magma underground. Sedimentary rocks are said to be clastic if they consist of particles of older rock (gravel), chemical if precipitated from solution (rock salt), or organic if formed from the remains or secretions of plants or animals (coal). Particles of lava exploded into the air during volcanic eruption may settle to the ground and form deposits of volcanic ash. Such rocks are called pyroclastics.

Solar System

The solar system is the group of celestial bodies, including the Earth, orbiting around and gravitationally bound by the star known as the sun, one of at least a hundred billion stars in our galaxy. Our solar system contains nine planets and one star. Mercury is the closest followed by Venus, Earth, Mars, Jupiter, Saturn, Uranus, Neptune, and Pluto. The Sun's retinue includes nine planets, at least 54 satellites, more than 1,000 observed comets, and thousands of lesser bodies known as asteroids, and meteoroids. All of these bodies are immersed in a tenuous sea of fragile and rocky interplanetary dust particles, perhaps ejected from comets at the time of their passage through the inner solar system or resulting from minor planet collisions. The sun is the only star

198

Science

known to be accompanied by such an extensive planetary system. A few nearby stars are now known to be encircled by swarms of particles of undetermined size, however, and evidence indicates that a number of stars are accompanied by giant planet like objects. Thus the possibility of a universe filled with many solar systems remains strong, though as yet unproven.

Solids-Gases-Liquids

Gases Gas molecules are very far apart. These molecules have no shape or size because as long as there is room they bounce radically.

Liquids Liquids molecules are free to roll and slide around each other. Although there is freedom of movement, these molecules do not bounce around as freely as gas molecules.

Solids These molecules don't move around freely. They do shake and vibrate to a small degree. There is a strong attraction or pull which keeps the molecules closely together. If molecules are heated they will vibrate faster and move apart.

Sound

The science, engineering, and art of the generation, propagation, and reception of sound waves constitute the subject of acoustics. The impact of the study of acoustics is extremely widespread. Acoustics is important, for example, in the fields of speech and hearing, the production of music, the design of theaters, the control of unwanted vibrations and noise in the environment, and medical diagnosis and therapy.

Stimulus-Response

When the mind is stimulated to give a certain response. Behaviorism is a 20th-century movement in psychology away from the study of consciousness and toward the study of physical acts. Motivated in part by the prolonged dispute among introspectionist psychologists as to whether there could be imageless thought, and inspired by the success of Ivan Pavlov's studies of conditioned reflexes, the American psychologist John Watson launched a campaign to turn psychology toward the study of behavior. Early studies focused on animal learning.

Stratosphere

The stratosphere is the second lowest of the four atmospheric layers. Its lower boundary is called the tropopause its upper boundary, the stratopause. The underlying troposphere is characterized by a vertical temperature gradient and thus vertical instability (weather changes). In contrast, temperatures in the stratosphere remain the same or even increase with increasing height, which indicates vertical stability. The stratospheric air flow is mainly horizontal. Ultraviolet absorption by ozone causes the high temperatures of the stratopause, which is usually between 48 and 53 km (30 and 33 mi) above the Earth's surface.

Thermosphere

The thermosphere is the highest and largest of the four atmospheric layers. It extends from the mesopause (about 80 km/50 mi above sea level), the average temperature is a low of -80 deg C (-112 deg F), to the thermopause (about 600 km/375 mi above sea level), where the temperature may reach highs of 225 deg C (440 deg F) at night during a period of minimum solar activity, and 1,475 deg C (2,690 deg F) in the daytime during a period of maximum solar activity. The upper part of the thermosphere is warm, because it readily absorbs solar ultraviolet radiation. The thermosphere is the only heterogeneous atmospheric layer. Vertical mixing takes place in the homosphere, the lowest 80 km (50 mi) of the thermosphere. Above the homosphere, however, position changes drastically, with gravity pulling the heavier gases (oxygen and nitrogen) toward the

Science

bottom of the thermosphere and consequently making helium and hydrogen the predominant particles in the top portion.

Tissue

Tissues are structured groupings of cells specialized to perform a common function necessary to the survival of the multicellular animal. Different tissues are needed so that the many abilities of the single-celled organism can be variously assigned to cells differentiated for that purpose. The process of tissue formation (histogenesis) evolves from the earlier process of cell differentiation. The fertilized ovum, a single cell, divides to form the blastula, in which tissues are not yet defined. As growth continues, the cells of the blastula begin to form the three germ layers, the ectoderm, mesoderm, and endoderm through the process of gastrulation.

Tornado

A tornado is a violent storm with whirling winds of up to 300 miles per hour. It appears as a rotating, funnel shaped cloud, from gray to black in color, which extends toward the ground from the base of a thundercloud. A tornado spins like a top and may sound like the roar of an airplane or that of a train. These short lived storms are the most violent and destructive of all atmospheric phenomena, and cover a small area. They frequently accompany the advance of hurricanes.

Troposphere

The troposphere is the lowest layer of the Earth's atmosphere. This is where important heat and water-vapor flux occur (usually upward during the day and downward during the night). Virtually all weather, or short-term variation in the atmosphere, occurs in the troposphere. The troposphere contains 99% of the atmosphere's water vapor and 90% of the air. Air temperature in the layer decreases with increasing height, except when inversions occur.

Science

Vertebrae or Spine

The spine, or spinal column, consists of bone and forms the primary support of the skeleton in vertebrates. The functions of the spine are to protect the spinal cord, roots of the spinal nerves, and attach the skull, ribs, pelvis, muscles, and ligaments. The flexible portion of the spine, or backbone, in humans consists of 24 individual vertebrae, 7 in the neck (cervical vertebrae), 12 in the thorax (thoracic vertebrae), and 5 in the lower back (lumbar vertebrae). The sacrum, located below the lumbar vertebrae and joined to the pelvis, consists of 5 fused vertebrae.

The coccyx, or tailbone, is located below the sacrum and consists of 3 to 5 fused, rudimentary vertebrae in humans. In general, the major part of a vertebra, the body, is a short, solid, cylindrical structure called the centrum. The remaining part is called the vertebral arch, or neural arch. The spinal cord passes through the large hole, or foramen, in the center of each vertebral arch of the spinal column. The foramen is continuous and protects the spinal cord and spinal fluid circulates within it. Spinal nerves pass from the cord through notches in the vertebral arch. A spiny projection extends from each side of the vertebral arch.

A third projection in the middle of the vertebral arch may be seen or felt through the skin. Thoracic vertebrae have articulating surfaces for attachment of ribs. The bodies of the vertebrae are separated from each other by cartilaginous pads called intervertebral disks. The vertebrae are held together by strong ligaments, but the general design of the spinal column allows considerable flexibility. The spine is subject to injury, curvature, arthritis, infections, and slipped disks.

Science

Volcano

A volcano is a vent in the Earth from which molten rock (magma) and gas erupt. The molten rock that erupts from the volcano (lava) forms a hill or mountain around the vent. The lava may flow out as a viscous liquid, or it may explode from the vent as solid or liquid particles.

Water Cycle

The water cycle starts with evaporation, then condensation, to precipitation, and finally runoff. The cycle will start again with evaporation.

Weather Forecasting

Forecasting weather (meteorology) is a major part of today's world. Because of the destructive power of many naturally occurring phenomena predicting the weather has saved many lives. The task of predicting the weather at a future time is called weather forecasting. As one of the primary objectives of the science of meteorology, weather forecasting has depended critically on the scientific and technological advances in meteorology that have taken place since the latter half of the 19th century.

Weathering

The breakdown of rock that takes place near the surface of the Earth. It involves both physical and chemical changes and is dependent on such factors as climate, vegetation, topography, and the composition of the rock.

Social Studies

Amendments

First Amendment
Gives all Americans the right to speak and worship freely. This amendment also gives Americans a free press as well as the right to gather (assemble) in a peaceful manner.

Second Amendment
Americans have the right to bear arms (weapons).

Third Amendment
During peacetime, soldiers cannot seek lodging in a private home without the owners consent.

Fourth Amendment
Without a legal warrant, the government cannot arrest, search, or take a persons belongings. This warrant must declare all intentions.

Fifth Amendment
A person suspected of a crime must be accused by a grand jury. It also states that a person will not be tried for the same crime twice or forced to give evidence against themselves.

Sixth Amendment
The right of a speedy trial and to be represented by council (lawyer).

Seventh Amendment
If a person sues another for more than $20 then that person has the right of a jury trial.

Eighth Amendment
A person accused of a crime shall be protected from unreasonable bails, fines, or cruel punishment.

Amendments

Ninth Amendment
Rights are protected against items not covered by the Constitution.

Tenth Amendment
The power not given by the Constitution to the federal government belongs to the states and the people.

11th Amendment (1795)
In order for a citizen to sue another person in federal court they must be from the same state.

12th Amendment (1804)
Provides for an electoral college to vote for President and Vice President. If no one candidate receives a majority then the House of Representatives will elect the President.

13th Amendment (1865)
Outlaws slavery in the United States.

14th Amendment (1868)
Former slaves are citizens and guarantees all citizens equal protection under the law.

15th Amendment (1870)
The right to vote cannot be denied because of race.

16th Amendment (1913)
Gives Congress the power to collect income taxes.

17th Amendment (1913)
United States Senators will be elected by the people and not state lawmakers.

Amendments

18th Amendment (1919)
Makes it illegal to make, sell, or transport liquor.

19th Amendment (1920)
Gives American women the right to vote.

20th Amendment (1933)
Changes the time when an elected American takes office (Congress and President).

21th Amendment (1933)
This amendment repeals the 18th Amendment.

22nd Amendment (1951)
A President can only be elected to no more than two terms.

23rd Amendment (1961)
Gives Americans living in the District of Columbia the right to vote for President and Vice President.

24th Amendment (1964)
Americans cannot be forced to pay a tax until they vote on it.

25th Amendment (1967)
States that the V. President will take over when the President can no longer continue in office.

26th Amendment (1971)
Gives citizens 18 years & older the right to vote.

27th Amendment (1992)
No law, varying the compensation for the services of the Senators and Representatives, shall take effect until an election of Representatives shall have intervened.

Explorers

Alexander the Great (356-323 BC) The king of Macedonia who led an expedition as far east as the Indus River. Expanded the knowledge of the western world about other civilizations.

Amundsen, Roald (1872-1928) A Norwegian explorer who was the first man to sail the Northwest Passage. He was also the first to reach the South Pole as well as the first to reach both Poles.

Armstrong, Neil (1930-) With fellow American Edwin Aldrin, landed on the surface of the moon July 20th, 1969.

Ashley, William (1778-1838) Revolutionized the fur trade by devising a rendezvous system in which company agents met independent trappers during the summer to exchange goods.

Back, George (1796-1878) A British naval officer who took part in four expeditions of the Canadian Arctic. He was the first European to see and travel down what is today called Back River.

Baffin, William (1584-1622) An Englishman that made two attempts to find the Northwest Passage to Asia.

Balboa, Vasco de Nunez (1475-1519) A Spanish explorer who crossed the Isthmus of Panama and the first European to see the Pacific Ocean.

Baranov, Alexander (1746-1819) A Russian trader responsible for much of the exploration of the Alaskan coast.

Bering, Vitus (1681-1741) A Danish navigator sailing for the Russian Tsar and one of the first to sail to North America.

Boone, Daniel (1734-1820) An American who was one of the first to explore Kentucky and founded the first American settlement west of the Appalachian Mountains.

Explorers

Bougainville, Louis Antoine (1729-1811) A French officer who led the first French circumnavigation of the globe.

Byrd, Richard (1888-1957) An American naval pilot who was the first to fly over the North and South Poles.

Byron, John (1723-1786) An English naval captain who claimed the Faulkland Islands for England then completed the voyage around the world.

Cabeza de Vaca, Alvar (1490-1556) A Spanish explorer who spent many years in Texas after being shipwrecked.

Cabot, John (1451-1498) An Italian navigator sailing in the service of England. He was believed to be the first to reach the mainland of North America following the Vikings.

Cabot, Sebastian (1484-1557) A Venetian navigator who explored the coast of North America for the king of England.

Cabrillo, Juan Rodriquez (1497-1543) A Portuguese explorer who was the first to explore the coast of California in the service of Spain.

Cano, Juan Sebastian (1519-1522) Took over after Megellan's death. On the last surviving ship, the Victoria, he returned to Spain by the way of the Cape of Good Hope. The first expedition to circumvent the world.

Carteret, Philip (1734-1796) A British naval officer who commanded a voyage around the world. First European to see many of the Pacific Islands.

Cartier, Jacques (1491-1557) A Frenchman who discovered the St. Lawrence River and the Gulf of St. Lawrence.

Explorers

Champlain, Samuel (1570-1635) A Frenchman who explored much of the eastern part of North America and helped found French colonies in Acadia and Quebec.

Clark, William (1770-1838) An American who was accompanied by Meriwether Lewis on the first American expedition from the Mississippi River to the Pacific Ocean.

Colter, John (1774-1813) An American fur trapper who was the first Westerner to see the Yellow Stone and Grand Teton Parks.

Columbus, Christopher (1451-1506) An Italian mariner that made several trips to the Caribbean and South America. Is credited with the discovery of the Americas and landed in the West Indies on October 12, 1492.

Cook, James (1728-1779) An English mariner who explored the Pacific Ocean, Antarctica, and the Arctic.

Coronado, Francisco Vazquez (1510-1554) A Spanish explorer who led the first European expedition to the Southwestern United States.

Corte-Real, Gaspar (1455-1501) Along with his brother, Miguel, explored the North Atlantic and Newfoundland area.

Cortes, Hernando (1485-1547) A Spanish conquistador who conquered Mexico and sponsored many expeditions in the Americas.

Cousteau, Jacques (1910-1998) Undoubtedly the most famous underwater explorer. He was a French naval officer and at one time, he invented the aqualung and designed the first underwater habitats.

Da Gama, Vasco (1460-1524) A Portuguese nobleman who led the first European expeditions around Africa to India.

Explorers

Davis, John (1550-1605) An Englishman who discovered the Faulkland Islands.

Soto, Hernando de (1500-1542) A Spaniard who led the first European expedition to the Southwestern United States.

Drake, Francis (1543-1596) An English seaman who was the second to sail around the world. He also led the English in defeating the Spanish Armada.

Dumont d'Urille, Jules Sebastian (1790-1842) A French naval officer who made several important scientific expeditions to the Pacific Ocean and was the first Frenchman to explore Antarctica.

Earhart, Amelia (1898-1937) The first American female pilot. She set numerous records, including being the first female to fly across the Atlantic. She disappeared in the Pacific while attempting to fly around the world (1937).

Eric the Red (950-1004) A Norsman who discovered Greenland (981) and was the first to settle in the new world.

Ericsson, Leif (975-1020) Son of Eric the Red, he sailed from Greenland to the coast of North America.

Fraser, Simon (1776-1862) An American born Canadian who discovered the Fraser River and opened up British Columbia to trade with Europe.

Fremont, John Charles (1813-1890) An American surveyor known as the "pathfinder" because he opened large parts of the American West for settlement.

Gagarin, Yuri (1934-1968) A Soviet cosmonaut who was the first human is space. He made one complete orbit on April 12, 1961.

Explorers

Gilbert, Humphrey (1539-1583)   An English nobleman who founded the first English colony in North America.

Glenn, John (1921-)   First American to orbit earth on February 20, 1961. Then he did it again in 1998!

Gray, Robert (1751-1792)   An American who discovered the Columbia River and Grays Harbor.

Groseilliers, Medard Chouart (1618-1696) A Frenchman who founded the Hudson's Bay Company and was responsible for opening up some of the main fur trading areas of North America.

Hearne, Samuel (1745-1792)   An English employee of the Hudson's Bay Company and was the first European to travel across the interior of Canada's Northwest Territories. He discovered the Coppermine River and reached the Arctic Ocean.

Hillary, Edmund (1919-) From New Zealand, he was the first person to climb Mt. Everest (May 29). He also led an expedition to the South Pole.

Hudson, Henry (-1611) An English navigator who led two expeditions to North America in search of the Northwest Passage. He also explored the Hudson River.

Hunt, Wilson (1782-1842) An American, along with Canadian Robert Stuart, pioneered the route through the northwestern United States that was to become known as the Oregon Trail.

Jolliet, Louis (1645-1700) A Frenchman who was the first to travel down the Mississippi River.

La Salle, Rene Cavelier de (1643-1687) A French adventurer who was the first to sail down the Mississippi River to its mouth.

211

Explorers

Lewis, Mariwether (1774-1809) An American who was accompanied by William Clark on the first American expedition from the Mississippi River to the Pacific Ocean.

Lindbergh, Charles (1902-1974) An American who was the first to fly across the Atlantic Ocean.

Livingston, David (1813-1873) A Scotsman who transversed South Africa discovering Lake Ngami, Zambezi River, Victoria Falls, Lakes Chilwa and Nyasa.

Magellan, Ferdinand (1480-1521) A Portuguese explorer who was in the service of Spain on an expedition around the world. Although he was killed in the Philippines, part of his expedition made the first encirclement of the world.

Markham, Beryl (1902-1986) Born in England, she was the first woman to fly from London to North America.

McClure, Robert (1807-1873) A British naval officer he was sent to find Sir John Franklin and discovered the Northwest Passage north of the American continent.

Nicollet, Jean (1598-1642) A Frenchman, he was the first European to travel through the Great Lakes to the states of Wisconsin and Illinois.

Peary, Robert (1856-1920) An American naval officer and the first person to reach the North Pole.

Pfeiffer, Ida (1797-1858) An Australian, she was the first woman to travel around the world alone. She did it twice.

Pinzon, Vicente (1463-1514) A Spaniard and a commander during Columbus's first voyage he made several voyages to America on his own. He discovered the Amazon River and Brazil.

Explorers

Pizarro, Francisco (1475-1541) A Spanish explorer, he led the first European expedition to Peru and he conquered the Inca Empire.

Polo, Marco (1254-1324)   An Italian that spent 24 years traveling throughout Asia in the court of Kublai Khan.

Ponce de Leon, Juan (1474-1521) A Spanish soldier and explorer he was the first European to visit Florida and looked for the *Fountain of Youth.*

Post, Wiley (1899-1935) An American who set a speed record for flying around the world and later became the first person to fly solo around the world.

Raleigh, Walter (1552-1618)   An English explorer who sponsored the first English settlement in North America and he led two expeditions to the Orinoco River in South America.

Ride, Sally (1951-) The first American woman in space, June 18, 1983.

Smith, Jedadiah (1799-1831) The first American to travel to the Southwestern United States that was, at the time, part of Mexico.

Smith, John (1606-1609) An English adventurer who took part in the first English colony in Virginia and led expeditions to the Chesapeake Bay and the coast of New England.

Teixeira, Pedro de (1587-1641) A Portuguese adventurer who made the first upstream trip on the Amazon River. He claimed the entire Amazon basin for Portugal.

Tereshkova, Valentina (1937-) A Soviet cosmonaut and the first woman in space.

Explorers

Thompson, David (1770-1857) An Englishman who explored much of northwestern Canada. He was the first person to travel through the Rocky Mountains to the Columbia River and down to its mouth.

Tonty, Henri de (1650-1704) A Frenchman who accompanied La Salle on his trip down the Mississippi River and led expeditions throughout the Mississippi Valley.

Urdaneta, Andres (1508-1568) A Spanish conquistador who established a colony in Chile and explored most of the country.

Valdivia, Pedro de (1500-1553) A Spaniard that explored Chile.

Vespucci, Amerigo (1451-1512) An Italian merchant who made two expeditions to the Americas which were later named in his honor.

Vancouver, George (1757-1798) A British naval officer who explored and mapped the coast of Northwestern America.

Vizcaino, Sebastian (1596-1603) A Spanish mariner explored the west coast of Mexico (Baja California). He sailed up to San Diego and Monterey Bays.

Wallace, Alfred (1823-1913) An Englishman who made two scientific expeditions to South America and formulated the modern theory of evolution at the same time as Charles Darwin.

Wallis, Samuel (1728-1795) An English naval captain who made a circumnavigation of the world and was the first European to visit the Tahiti Islands.

Yeager, Charles (1923-) An American fighter pilot and later a test pilot, he was the first to fly faster then the speed of sound on October 14th, 1947.

Presidents

George Washington *1789-1797* (Federalist)
VP John Adams
Born Feb. 22, 1732 in Pope's Creek, Virginia; Died Dec. 14
1799 of pneumonia; Married to: Martha Dandrige Custis.
During his life he was trained as a surveyor. He became
commander of the American army during the Revolutionary
War and was chairman of the Constitutional Convention.

John Adams *1797-1801* (Federalist)
VP Thomas Jefferson
Born Oct. 19, 1735 in Braintree, Massachusetts; Died July 4,
1825 of natural causes. Married to: Abigail Smith. He
studied at Harvard University and practiced law. He was
also the first Vice President as well as the first president to
live in the White House.

Thomas Jefferson *1801-1809* (Democratic-Republican)
VP Aaron Burr (1801-1805) George Clinton (1805-1809)
Born Apr. 13, 1743 in Shadwell, Virginia; Died July 4, 1826
of natural causes. Married to Martha Wayles Skelton. He
studied at William and Mary and practiced law. He wrote
the Declaration of Independence & was the first secretary
of state. His purchase of the Louisiana territory doubled
the size of the United States.

James Madison *1809-1817* (Democratic-Republican)
VP George Clinton (1809-1812) Elbridge Gerry (1813-1817)
Born Mar. 16, 1751 in Port Conway, Virginia; Died June 28,
1836 of natural causes. Married to Dorothea Payne Todd.
He studied at Princeton University (College of New Jersey)
and practiced law. He helped with the Constitution and
during the War of 1812 had to flee the White House when
the British attached.

215

Presidents

James Monroe *1817-1825* (Democratic-Republican)
VP Daniel Tompkins
Born Apr. 28, 1758 in Westmoreland, Virginia; Died July 4, 1831 of natural causes. Married to Elizabeth Kortright. He studied law at William and Mary. During his career he was a congressman, senator, and Secretary of State. With the Monroe Doctrine, he warned Europe to stay out of American affairs.

John Q. Adams *1825-1829* (National Republican)
VP John Calhoun
Born July 11, 1767 in Braintree, Massachusetts; Died Feb. 23, 1848 of a stroke. Married to Louisa Johnson. He studied law at Harvard University. He was senator and Secretary of State.

Andrew Jackson *1829-1837* (Democrat)
VP 's
John Calhoun (1829-1832) Martin Van Buren (1833-1837)
Born Mar. 15, 1767 in The Waxhaws, South Carolina; Died June 8, 1845 of natural causes. Married to Rachel Robards. He was a hero of the War of 1812. He was a senator and congressman. He established the "spoils system" that rewarded supporters by giving them government jobs.

Martin Van Buren *1837-1841* (Democrat)
VP Richard Johnson
Born Dec. 5, 1782 in Kinderhook, New York; Died July 24, 1862 of natural causes. Married to Hannah Hoes. He was a state public official, senator, governor of NY, and Secretary of State. He was president during a period of economic hard times.

Presidents

William Harrison *1841* (Whig)

VP John Tyler

Born Feb. 9, 1773 in Berley, Virginia; Died Apr. 4, 1841 of pneumonia. Married to Anna Tuthill Symes. He served in the War of 1812. He was the governor of the Indiana Territory, congressman, and a senator.

John Tyler *1841-1845* (Whig)

VP None

Born Mar. 29, 1790 in Greenway, Virginia; Died Jan. 18, 1862 of bronchitis. Married to Letitia Christian (1st); Julia Gardiner (2nd). Attended William and Mary and practiced law. He was a congressman, senator, Governor, and Secretary of State. Signed the bill that allowed Texas to join the union.

James K. Polk *1845-1849* (Democrat)

VP George Dallas

Born Nov. 2, 1795 in Mecklenberg, North Carolina; Died June 15, 1849 of heart failure. Married to Sarah Childress. He graduated from North Carolina University and practiced law. He was Speaker of the House and governor of Tennessee. He sent troops to begin the Mexican War & gain territory in the southwest.

Zachary Taylor *1849-1850* (Whig)

VP Millard Fillmore

Born Nov. 24, 1784 in Orange County, Virginia; Died July 9, 1850 of cholera. Married to Margaret Smith. Mexican War hero and nicknamed "Old Rough & Ready".

Presidents

Millard Fillmore *1850-1853* (Whig)

VP None
Born Jan. 7, 1800 in Locke, New York; Died Mar. 8, 1874 of a stroke. Married to Abigail Powers (1st); Caroline McIntosh (2nd). He taught in country schools & practiced law. He was a NY State legislator and congressman. He favored the Compromise of 1850 to settle the dispute over slavery in newly settled territory.

Franklin Pierce *1853-1857* (Democrat)

VP William King
Born Nov. 23, 1804 in Hillsboro, New Hampshire; Died Oct. 8, 1869 of natural causes. Married to Jane Appleton. He went to Bowdoin College and practiced law. He served in the Mexican War. Signed the Kansas-Nebraska Act which placed slavery under local law.

James Buchanan *1857-1861* (Democrat)

VP John Breckinridge
Born Apr. 23, 1791 in Cove Cap, Pennsylvania; Died June 1, 1868 of natural causes. Never married. Graduated from Dickson College and practiced law. Served in the War of 1812 and was a congressman, Minister to Russia and Britain, senator, and Secretary of State. Wanted popular sovereignty, vote of the people, to settle the slavery question in new states.

Abraham Lincoln *1861-1865* (Republican)

VP's Hannibal Hamlin (1861-1865), Andrew Johnson (1865)
Born Feb. 12, 1809 in Hardin County, Kentucky; Died Apr. 15, 1865 assassinated. Married to Mary Todd. Was an Illinois state legislator and congressman. Signed the Emancipation Proclamation to free the slaves.

Presidents

Andrew Johnson *1865-1869* (Democrat)
VP None
Born Dec. 29, 1808 in Raleigh, North Carolina; Died July 31, 1875 of a stroke. Married to Eliza McCardle. He was a congressman, governor of Tennessee, senator. The only president ever impeached. Charged with conspiring against congress. He was not convicted.

Ulysses S. Grant *1869-1877* (Republican)
VP Schuyler Colfax (1869-1873) Henry Wilson (1873-1877)
Born Apr. 27, 1822 in Point Pleasant, Ohio; Died July 23, 1885 of throat cancer. Married to Julia Dent. Graduated from the US Military Academy at WEST POINT. He served in the Mexican war and was commander of the Union Forces in the Civil War. He supported the 15th amendment.

Rutherford B. Hayes *1877-1881* (Republican)
VP William A. Wheeler
Born Oct. 4, 1822 in Delaware, Ohio; Died Jan. 17, 1893 of natural causes. Married to Lucy Webb. Graduated from Kenyon College and Harvard Law School. Congressman and governor of Ohio. He won the presidency in a disputed election. Ended troop occupation of Southern states ending Reconstruction.

James A. Garfield *1881* died (Republican)
VP Chester A. Arthur
Born Nov. 19, 1831 in Orange, Ohio; Died Sep. 19, 1881 assassinated. Married to Lucretia Rudolph. Graduated from Williams College and taught school. Served in Civil War. Congressman, fought against "spoils system" assassinated after 6 months in office.

219

Presidents

Chester A. Arthur *1881-1885* (Republican)
VP None
Born October 5, 1829 In North Fairfield Vermont; Died November 18, 1886. Assumed office after James Garfield died in office. Married Ellen Herndon.

Grover Cleveland *1885-1889/1893-1897* (Democrat)
VP 's
Thomas Hendricks (1885) Adlai Stevenson (1893-1897)
Born Mar. 18, 1837 in Caldwell, New Jersey; Died June 24, 1908 of natural causes. Married to Frances Folsom.

Benjamin Harrison *1889-1893* (Republican)
VP Levi Morton
Born Aug. 20, 1833 in North Bend, Ohio; Died March 13, 1901 of natural causes. Married to Caroline Scott.

William McKinley *1897-1901* (Republican)
VP's
Garrett Hobart (1897-1899) Theodore Roosevelt (1901)
Born Jan. 29, 1843 in Niles, Ohio; Died Sep. 14, 1901 assassinated. Married to Isa Saxton.

Theodore Roosevelt *1901-1909* (Republican)
VP Charles Fairbanks (1905-1909)
Born Oct. 27, 1858 in New York, New York; Died Jan. 6, 1919 of heart failure. Married to Alice Lee (1st); Edith Carow (2nd).

Presidents

William H. Taft *1909-1913* (Republican)
VP James Sherman
Born Sep. 15, 1857 in Cincinnati, Ohio; Died Mar. 8, 1930 of heart failure. Married to Helen Herron.

Woodrow Wilson *1913-1921* (Democrat)
VP Thomas Marshall
Born Dec. 28, 1856 in Staunton, Virginia; Died Feb. 3, 1924 of natural causes. Married-Ellen Axson (1st); Edith Galt (2nd).

Warren G. Harding *1921-1923* (Republican)
VP Calvin Coolidge
Born Nov. 2, 1865 in Blooming Grove, Ohio; Died Aug. 2, 1923 of a stroke. Married to Florence DeWolfe.

Calvin Coolidge *1923-1929* (Republican)
VP Charles Dawes
Born July 4, 1872 in Plymouth Notch, Vermont; Died Jan. 5, 1933 of heart failure. Married to Grace Goohue.

Herbert Hoover *1929-1933* (Republican)
VP Charles Curtis
Born Aug. 10, 1874 in West Branch, Iowa; Died Oct. 20, 1964 of natural causes. Married to Lou Henry.

Franklin D. Roosevelt *1933-1945* (Democrat)
VP John Garner (1933-1941) Henry Wallace (1941-1945) Harry Truman (1945) Born Jan. 30, 1882 in Hyde Park New York; Died Apr. 12, 1945 of a cerebral hemorrhage. Married to Anna Eleanor.

Presidents

Harry S. Truman *1945-1953* (Democrat)
VP Alben Barkey
Born May 8, 1884 in Lamar, Missouri; Died Dec. 26, 1972 of natural causes. Married to Elizabeth Wallace.

Dwight D. Eisenhower *1953-1961* (Republican)
VP Richard Nixon
Born Oct. 14, 1890 in Denison, Texas; Died Mar. 28, 1969 of heart failure. Married to Mamie Doud.

John F. Kennedy *1961-1963* (Democrat)
VP Lyndon Johnson
Born May 29, 1917 in Brookline, Massachusetts; Died Nov. 22, 1963 assassinated. Married to Jacqueline Bouvier.

Lyndon B. Johnson *1963-1969* (Democrat)
VP Hubert Humphrey
Born Aug. 27, 1908 in Stonewall, Texas; Died Jan. 22, 1973 of natural causes. Married to Claudia Alta Taylor.

Richard M. Nixon *1969-1974* (Republican)
VP's
Spiro Agnew (1969-1973) Gerald Ford (1973-1974)
Born Jan. 9, 1913 in Yorba Linda, California; Died 1995. Married to Patricia Ryan.

Gerald R. Ford *1974-1977* (Republican)
VP Nelson Rockefeller
Born July 14, 1913 in Omaha, Nebraska. Married to Betty Bloomer.

Presidents

Jimmy E. Carter *1977-1981* (Democrat)
  VP Walter Mondale
  Born Oct. 1, 1924 in Plains, Georgia. Married to Rosalynn Smith

Ronald W. Reagan *1981-1989* (Republican)
  VP George Bush
  Born Feb. 6, 1911 in Tampico Illinois. Married to Nancy Davis.

George H. W. Bush *1989-1993* (Republican)
  VP Dan Quayle
  Born June 12, 1924 in Milton, Massachusetts. Married to Barbara Pierce.

William Clinton *1993-2000* (Democrat)
  VP Al Gore
  Born August 19, 1946 in Hope Arkansas. Married to Hillary Rodham.

United States
Indicates one of the original 13 states

Alabama (1819)
HEART OF DIXIE STATE
Capital-Montgomery
Area: 51,705 square miles
Population: 4,040,587

Alaska (1959)
LAND OF THE MIDNIGHT
SUN
Capital: Juneau
Area: 591,004 square miles
Population: 550,043

Arizona (1912)
GRAND CANYON STATE
Capital-Phoenix
Area: 114,000 square miles
Population: 3,665,228

Arkansas (1836)
LAND OF OPPORTUNITY
Capital-Little Rock
Area: 53,187 square miles
Population: 2,350,725

California (1850)
THE GOLDEN STATE
Capital-Sacramento
Area: 158,706 square miles
Population: 29,760,021

Colorado (1867)
CENTENNIAL STATE
Capital-Denver
Area: 104,091 square miles
Population: 3,294,394

Connecticut (1788)*
CONSTITUTION STATE
Capital-Hartford
Area: 5,018 square miles
Population: 3,287,116

Delaware (1787)*
THE FIRST STATE
Capital-Dover
Area: 2,044 square miles
Population: 666,168

Florida (1845)
SUNSHINE STATE
Capital-Tallahassee
Area: 58,664 square miles
Population: 12,937,926

Georgia (1788)*
THE PEACH STATE
Capital-Atlanta
Area: 58,910 square miles
Population: 6,478,216

United States
Indicates one of the original 13 states

Hawaii (1959)
ALOHA STATE
Capital-Honolulu
Area: 6,471 square miles
Population: 1,108,229

Idaho (1890)
GEM STATE
Capital-Boise
Area: 83,564 square miles
Population: 1,006,749

Illinois (1818)
LAND OF LINCOLN
Capital-Springfield
Area: 56,400 square miles
Population: 11,430,602

Indiana (1816)
HOOSIER STATE
Capital-Indianapolis
Area: 36,185 square miles
Population: 5,544,159

Iowa (1846)
HAWKEYE STATE
Capital-Des Moines
Area: 56,275 square miles
Population: 2,776,755

Kansas (1861)
SUNFLOWER STATE
Capital-Topeka
Area: 82,277 square miles
Population: 2,477,574

Kentucky (1792)
BLUE GRASS STATE
Capital-Frankfort
Area: 40,409 square miles
Population: 3,685,296

Louisiana (1812)
BAYOU STATE
Capital-Baton Rouge
Area: 47,752 square miles
Population: 4,219,973

Maine (1870)
PINE TREE STATE
Capital-Augusta
Area: 33,265
Population: 1,227,928

Maryland (1788)*
FREE STATE
Capital-Annapolis
Area: 10,460 square miles
Population: 4,781,468

United States
Indicates one of the original 13 states

Massachusetts (1788)*
BAY STATE
Capital-Boston
Area: 8,284 square miles
Population: 6,016,425

Michigan (1837)
WOLVERINE STATE
Capital-Lansing
Area: 58,527 square miles
Population: 9,295,297

Minnesota (1858)
GOPHER STATE
Capital-Saint Paul
Area: 84,402 square miles
Population: 4,375,099

Mississippi (1817)
MAGNOLIA STATE
Capital-Jackson
Area: 47,689 square miles
Population: 2,573,216

Missouri (1821)
'SHOW ME' STATE
Capital-Jefferson City
Area: 69,697 square miles
Population: 5,117,073

Montana (1889)
TREASURE STATE
Capital-Helena
Area: 147,046 square miles
Population: 799,065

Nebraska (1867)
CORN HUSKER STATE
Capital-Lincoln
Area: 77,355 square miles
Population: 1,578,385

Nevada (1864)
SILVER STATE
Capital-Carson City
Area: 110,561 square miles
Population: 1,201,833

New Hampshire (1788)*
GRANITE STATE
Capital-Concord
Area: 9,279 square miles
Population: 1,109,252

New Jersey (1787)*
GARDEN STATE
Capital-Trenton
Area: 7,787 square miles
Population: 7,730,188

United States
Indicates one of the original 13 states

New Mexico (1912)
LAND OF ENCHANTMENT
Capital-Santa Fe
Area: 121,593 square miles
Population: 1,515,069

New York (1788)*
EMPIRE STATE
Capital-Albany
Area: 49,108 square miles
Population: 17,990,455

North Carolina (1789)*
TAR HEEL STATE
Capital-Raleigh
Area: 52,669 square miles
Population: 6,628,637

North Dakota (1889)
SIOUX STATE
Capital-Bismarck
Area: 70,702 square miles
Population: 638,800

Ohio (1803)
BUCKEYE STATE
Capital-Columbus
Area: 41,330 square miles
Population: 10,847,115

Oklahoma (1907)
SOONER STATE
Capital-Oklahoma City
Area: 69,956 square miles
Population: 3,145,585

Oregon (1859)
BEAVER STATE
Capital-Salem
Area: 97,073 square miles
Population: 2,842,321

Pennsylvania (1787)*
KEYSTONE STATE
Capital-Harrisburg
Area: 45,308 square miles
Population: 11,881,643

Rhode Island (1790)*
LITTLE RHODY
Capital-Providence
Area: 1,212 square miles
Population: 1,003.464

South Carolina (1889)*
COYOTE STATE
Capital-Columbia
Area: 31,113 square miles
Population: 3,486,703

United States
Indicates one of the original 13 states

South Dakota (1889)
PALMETTO STATE
Capital-Pierre
Area: 77,116 square miles
Population: 696,004

Tennessee (1796)
VOLUNTEER STATE
Capital-Nashville
Area: 42,144 square miles
Population: 4,877,185

Texas (1845)
LONE STAR STATE
Capital-Austin
Area: 266,807 square miles
Population: 16,986,510

Utah (1896)
BEEHIVE STATE
Capital-Salt Lake City
Area: 84,899 square miles
Population: 1,722,850

Vermont (1791)
GREEN MOUNTAIN STATE
Capital-Montpelier
Area: 9,614 square miles
Population: 562,758

Virginia (1788)*
THE OLD DOMINION
Capital-Richmond
Area: 40,817 square miles
Population: 6,187,358

Washington (1889)
EVERGREEN STATE
Capital-Olympia
Area: 68,139 square miles
Population: 4,866,692

West Virginia (1863)
MOUNTAIN STATE
Capital-Charleston
Area: 24,231 square miles
Population: 1,793,477

Wisconsin (1848)
BADGER STATE
Capital-Madison
Area: 56,153 square miles
Population: 4,891,769

Wyoming (1890)
EQUALITY STATE
Capital-Cheyenne
Area: 97,809 square miles
Population: 453,588

Timeline

1492 On October 12th Columbus arrives in the New World (West Indies) on board the *Santa Maria* with the *Nina* and *Pinta*.

1523 Giovanni de Verrazano reaches the coast of New York.

1534 Jacques Cartier begins the exploration of the St. Lawrence River.

1607 Founding of Jamestown by Christopher Newport.

1620 Pilgrims arrive at Cape Cod on board the Mayflower.

1673 Marquette and Joliet reach the mouth of the Mississippi River.

1718 Bienville founds New Orleans.

1733 Oglethorpe founds Georgia.

1766 Repeal of the Stamp Act.

1770 Boston Massacre!

1773 Boston Tea Party: Americans boarded British ships and dumped tea overboard protesting tax policies.

1774 First Continental Congress.

1775 Revolutionary War begins.

1775 Battle of Bunker Hill.

1776 The 13 colonies declare their independence from England on July 4th and adopt the Declaration of Independence.

1781 Cornwallis surrenders at Yorktown.

Timeline

1783   Treaty of Varsilles, Britain recognizes the United States.

1787   Philadelphia Convention, the establishment of the federal government.

1791   Jefferson forms the Democratic Party.

1803   Louisiana Purchase: Napoleon was about to go to war with England. He needed money so Jefferson purchases territory from Napoleon for $15,000,000.

1804   Lewis and Clark begin their journey through the newly purchased Louisiana territory.

1807   Aaron Burr tried for treason.

1807   The Embargo Act

1808   The repeal of the Embargo Act.

1812   The War of 1812 with Britain begins on June 18.

1815   On January 8th, Andrew Jackson and his troops won the battle of New Orleans.

1818   Spain cedes Florida to the United States.

1819   First steamship crosses the Atlantic Ocean.

1820   Missouri Compromise

1823   Monroe Doctrine

1825   Completion of the Erie Canal.

1830   The Great Debate between Daniel Webster and Robert Hayne.

Timeline

1835   Samuel Colt submits a patent for his revolver.

1836   Alamo: This mission in San Antonio was the site of the famous battle where all the defenders, including Jim Bowie and Davy Crockett, were killed.

1836   Republic of Texas established.

1837   Samuel Morse develops the telegraph.

1846   Sewing machine invented.

1847   Gold rush in California.

1847   Conquest of California.

1850   Clay Compromise

1854   Kansas-Nebraska Act repealed the Missouri Compromise.

1854   Founding of the Republican Party.

1857   The Dread Scott decision.

1858   The Lincoln-Douglas debate.

1859   First oil well drilled.

1859   John Brown's Raid

1861   Eleven southern states succeed from the Union forming the Confederate States of America.

1861   Civil War begins!

1863   Emancipation Proclamation

Timeline

1865   Lee surrenders to Grant at Appomattox Court House on April 9th. This marks the end of the Civil War!

1865   President Lincoln assassinated at Ford's Theater.

1867   The United States purchases Alaska from Russia for $7,200,000. Also known as Seward's Folly.

1867   Reconstruction Act, March 2nd.

1868   Impeachment trial of Andrew Jackson.

1869   The first transcontinental railroad is completed.

1873   The Great Bonanza, silver is discovered in Nevada.

1873   Kindergarten is introduced in St. Louis.

1876   On February 15 a patent was awarded for the manufacture of barbed wire.

1876   Bell invents the telephone

1879   Edison invents the electric lamp.

1879   Salvation Army comes to America from England.

1881   The American Red Cross Society is organized with Clara Burton as president.

1895   Marconi invents the wireless telegraph.

1898   The Spanish American War begins.

1903   Wright brothers fly at Kitty Hawk.

1908   William Peary becomes the first person to reach the North Pole.

Timeline

1908   Henry Ford develops the Model T.

1909   Mass production of the Ford Model T car begins.

1913   Federal Reserve Act enacted.

1914   Assassination of Archduke Francis Ferdinand on June 28th starts the first Word War.

1914   Panama Canal opens.

1917   The United States enter WW I.

1918   Sergeant Alvin York wins the Congressional Medal of Honor.

1918   On November 11th, WW I ends. The armistice was signed on November 11th at 11:00 am signifying the end of WW I.

1919   Treaty of Versailles is signed but the United States Senate rejected the treaty.

1919   Paris Peace Conference begins in January.

1927   Charles Lindbergh flies across the Atlantic.

1929   On September 29th, the stock market crashes.

1930   Wiley Post flies round the world.

1939   On September 1st the Germans invaded Poland to start the second world war.

1940   On May 10 Germany invades France and what seemed to be one of the strongest armies in the world was overrun in one month.

Timeline

1941 At 7:55 am the Japanese started bombing Pearl Harbor. This action brought the United States into World War II.

1942 The Japanese capture the Philippine Islands.

1942 Bataan death march in the Philippine Islands.

1944 On June 6th the battle for Europe begins (D-Day). American troops land on the coast of Normandy at Utah and Omaha beach.

1944 The "Battle of the Bulge" was the largest tank battle of World War II.

1945 Yalta Conference

1945 Roosevelt dies on April 12.

1945 Germany and Italy surrender to the Allies.

1945 Audie Murphy, America's most decorated soldier, receives the Medal of Honor.

1945 On August 6th and 9th the United States dropped the first atomic bombs on Hiroshima and Nagasaki.

1945 Japan surrenders on September 2nd on board the battleship Missouri.

1947 Chuck Yeagar breaks the sound barrier in the X-1.

1950 The United States enters the Korean War.

1950 North Atlantic Treaty Organization (NATO) established.

1951 General MacArthur relieved of command.

1953 Polio vaccine introduced by Jonas Salk.

1953 Marshall Plan

Timeline

1957   The first unmanned spacecraft (Sputnik) was placed in orbit.

1961   John Glenn becomes the first American to orbit the Earth.

1962   Cuban Missile Crisis

1963   On November 22nd, John F. Kennedy was assassinated in Dallas Texas.

1969   On July 20th Neil Armstrong becomes the first human to set foot on the Moon.

1975   The Viking spacecraft launched to explore Mars.

1977   Voyager 1 is launched to explore Jupiter. Voyager 2 was later launched to continue the mission in exploring Jupiter as well as Saturn, Uranus, and finally Neptune.

1981   The space shuttle, Columbia, rocketed into space.

1981   President Reagan assassination attempt.

1983   Sally Ride was the first American woman in space aboard the space shuttle (June 18).

1986   Space shuttle Challenger explodes.

1989   The Berlin Wall comes down.

1998   John Glenn rockets back into space after 37 years.

1999   William Clinton becomes only the second president to be impeached by the House of Representatives.

Index

Index

Index

Index

Index

Index

Index

Notes